Hot Flash Financial

Hot Flash Financial

*If you have hot flashes,
you have found the right book.*

WENDY WEISS

Copyright © 2013 by Wendy Weiss
All rights reserved. No part of this publication may be reproduced, stored in a retrieval system, or transmitted, in any form or by any means, electronic, mechanical, photocopying, recording, or otherwise, without the prior written permission of the author.

For information, visit hotflashfinancial.com
or address the author at info@hotflashfinancial.com.

ISBN 978-0-578-12239-7
Printed in the United States of America

Cover design: Deborah Perdue, Illumination Graphics
Book design: Lisa Diercks/Endpaper Studio
Text set in FF Celeste

IMAGE CREDITS: Cover image: Shutterstock; p. 8 (both): © Patrick/Fotosearch; p. 9: © Hill Street Studios/Corbis; p. 10: © P. Wei/iStockphoto; p. 16: © creatista/Fotosearch; p. 18 (top): © AJevs/iStockphoto; p. 18 (bottom): © creatista/Fotosearch; p. 20: © LisaFX/iStockphoto; p. 22: © aldomurillo/iStockphoto; p. 24: © Steve Cole/iStockphoto; p. 25: © tomprout/iStockphoto; p. 26: © DRB Images/iStockphoto; p. 29: © VILevi/iStockphoto; p. 32: © SDenisov/iStockphoto; p. 33: © LifesizeImages/iStockphoto; p. 41: © SarapulSar38/iStockphoto; p. 42: © sqback/iStockphoto; p. 46: © c8501089/iStockphoto; p. 50: © VikramRaghuvanshi/iStockphoto; p. 54: © Juanmonino/iStockphoto; p. 55: © Arsgera/iStockphoto; p. 56: © vm/iStockphoto; p. 64: © FredFroese/iStockphoto; p. 68: © Roel Smart/iStockphoto; p. 73: © GlobalStock/iStockphoto; p. 74: © esolla/iStockphoto; p. 80: © EMPPhotography/iStockphoto; p. 82: © Neustockimages/iStockphoto; p. 89: © DRB Images/iStockphoto; p. 91: © Mark Bowden/iStockphoto; p. 92: © Viorika/iStockphoto; p. 98: © elmvilla/iStockphoto; p. 99: © JacobH/iStockphoto; p. 100: © LisaFX/iStockphoto; p. 108: © kali9/iStockphoto; p. 128: © monkeybusinessimages/iStockphoto; p. 132: © Roel Smart/iStockphoto

This book is written for Women, of a certain age, And Distinction

Contents

Introduction   1

CHAPTER 1. If You Have Hot Flashes . . .   7

CHAPTER 2. Girl, Let's Talk   15

CHAPTER 3. It's Probably Not as Bad as You Think   31

CHAPTER 4. Are There "Unsightly Wrinkles" in Your Financial Future?   53

CHAPTER 5. We Have a Face Lift (for Your Finances)   67

CHAPTER 6. We Can Give You Lots of Options and More Control   87

CHAPTER 7. Okay, My Hot Flash Mama, You Accomplished a Lot!   103

Glossary   107

Resources   123

Hot Flash Extra! New Business Do's and Don'ts   133

About the Author   136

Introduction

I t was a *flash* of inspiration—a **hot flash,** in fact—that got me to write this book.

I realized that women, *like you and me*—**smart women—don't know enough about our money** and our future. But we need to. Really!

That's why I created *Hot Flash Financial.*

What is that? Well, it is a wacky approach developed by a highly trained financial adviser. (More on that—on *me!*—later.) It is designed to keep you laughing while you are learning new ideas and new skills—money skills. It focuses on getting **you** more **organized** and, at the same time, **knowledgeable.** *Hot Flash Financial* wants to give you **more control** over your life as well as **more security.**

I start by joking about hot flashes. I mean, they really are pretty funny (for most of us). They are unlike most other biological functions—eating, digesting, and so forth. They are simply dysfunctional! *Whew!* You have to stop anything you are doing to grab a fan or a glass of ice cold water. (I once watched a colleague, who had recently undergone chemotherapy, take off her wig—and reveal her bald head—in a big professional meeting because her hot flashes were so bad.) So hot flashes give us great material for a lot of jokes.

I then discuss key money issues, and I do so in a way that I think you will like. I *use laughter* to reduce the stress and anxiety that many of us feel when we start to think about money. And I get to jest about girl stuff—wrinkles and face lifts, marriage and money, diets and middle-aged bodies, and, of course, hot flashes.

Then I squeeze in some other stuff—the "financial" part.

But, you might respond, you use the term *financial*?!

Yes, I know. The word "financial" sounds soooo inscrutable, so mysterious and impenetrable. Anything related to finance seems to include all those words that can scare you off.

Remember, however, that you don't need to know everything about finance to improve your own security, just as you don't need to know everything about nutrition to eat well. Just learn a few new concepts and a few tricks by following a set of steps. It is that easy.

Hot Flash Financial **helps you** by explaining key concepts and, hopefully, inspiring you to act. As you read more and take our STEPS, you will feel *more capable* and enjoy greater control over your money. Your anxieties about your finances and your future will decrease. And your sense of power will increase. As *Hot Flash Financial* increases your knowledge and power, you will be able to make more intelligent decisions about your money and your future.

> *The more **control** you have over your money, the more **empowered** you will feel.* **Your stress and fear will start to melt away.**

I am going to start by asking you to get more organized. That's not so bad, is it? It's not so scary either, right? I know you can get organized. (If you can go out and buy plastic boxes to organize mountains and closets of "stuff," you can work with me.)

And I explain things clearly. I really encourage you to try some new skills—important ones, like reading an account statement. Don't worry, I will hold your hand and make you giggle while you practice doing this.

So keep reading.

By why on earth would you listen to me?

Who Am I? And Why Would You Ever Trust Me to Explain This to You?

The author is a bit shy and doesn't like to toot her own horn. But she—oops—*I* can teach you.

Why?

Well, I have an **MBA** in finance. And I also have **PhD**. That's the truth.

I have been working in finance and helping women with financial plans since 2001. I have published articles, authored blogs, been invited to "guest blog" for other sites, and taught courses to increase financial literacy. I even conducted research to understand why women avoided, ignored, or were too frightened and worried to focus on their money and the future.

What I found out while working with women is that we avoid the topic of finance like the plague. We often don't even like to think about it. Talking about money makes us feel stress, anxiety, fear. So we need a tension release.

I decided that tension release has to be **laughter!**

So I created *Hot Flash Financial*. I picked a name that brings a smile to most women's faces, if not outright giggles. And I bring humor to the discussion as frequently as possible. Read my funny explanations. Laugh at my metaphors. Take my quizzes. **Laugh and learn.** Work with me, please.

Shucks, I just wanna help you and become your best girlfriend. No, make that your BFF—**best financial friend**—when it comes to money issues. The one you turn to when you want to know something important about money or when you feel confused but want to change all that. **I will make things clear *and* cheer you on** as you practice these new skills. That way you will improve your finances and gain confidence. Each time you take a *Hot Flash Financial* STEP, you will feel you have more control. You will make better decisions about your money and your future. As a result, you will greatly improve your financial security.

Ready to work with me and *Hot Flash Financial*?

> *I promise I will give you* **intelligent advice** *so you can make good,* **informed decisions** *about* **your money** *and your* **future** *as well as take crucial steps to* **improve** *your* **security.**

Will you let *Hot Flash Financial* into your life? Gee, I hope so.

We can do it, girl—**together**.

Don't let it just be me yacking at you, or sitting on a bookshelf. Let's work together. Let me and *Hot Flash Financial* into your life. And have some fun along the way.

CHAPTER 1

If You Have Hot Flashes . . .

CHAPTER 1 GOALS

I am going to get you to smile and maybe even laugh. I will explain what hot flashes are for. Then I will reveal the goal of **Hot Flash Financial**. *I just want to help* **you** *become more financially secure.*

Y ou have received a **SIGN**.
What kind of a SIGN?

Well, I want you to see that hot flashes are really

- gentle **reminders** and encouragements,
- more direct **prompts,** and
- sometimes even **nags**

telling you *it is time* to learn more about your money and your future. Your hot flashes are saying that you need to take some important steps to make yourself more *financially secure.*

Hot flashes are also telling you that there is *no more time* to

- put it off,
- say you are too busy, or
- find any *other* reason to procrastinate.

Nope. Ya gotta start *now*.
    Why? Because it is *your future.* And *only you* can make it better.
    So let's work together.

Now, I know when I talk about money, you might feel a little stress. So I'll make sure I include a tension release: laughter.

> *Can we **laugh** here?*
> *You bet!*
> *This wouldn't be worth doing if we couldn't laugh a bit or even giggle throughout this process, especially when we tackle the tough stuff.*

I want to give you

- **less stress,**
- more **laughter,** and
- **control** over your money and your life.

What Is the *Hot Flash Financial* Goal?

Financial security for you
"So," you might ask, "what is financial security?"

> *Well, it is **not** being rich.*
> *Forget rich! It is probably too late to be that.*
> *Let's get real—and get security.*

Financial security is the feeling of safety and confidence that comes from knowing that you have enough money to pay for everything you need today ... and in your future. There is another important side to financial security: it gives you independence and a sense of dignity.

The feeling of independence and the safety associated with security probably sound good. So does dignity. I suspect you might like to have all of that.

Hot Flash Financial wants *you* to **take steps to increase your financial security.** So I give you the tools you need to help *you* improve your life.

I know you are smart and capable—after all, you made it this far! And, as they say, you are older and wiser now. You sure do have a lot of experience—and experience is a great teacher. So let's work with these strengths, *your* very own strengths.

This is, of course, a DIY (do it yourself) book. So you know what comes next: I ask you to **ACT!** I give you a set of STEPS you can use to make *yourself* stronger, safer, more secure.

> **Hot Flash Financial** *gives you to the STEPS that will guide you to*
> • *make* **your** *life and* **your future** *one of* **dignity** *and* **security** *and*
> • *make your future one of* **economic independence.**
> *If you take my STEPS, you can enjoy the freedom from worry that financial security brings.*

Your first STEP doesn't need to be "perfect." In fact, your second and third STEPS don't need to be perfect either. **Perfection is not our goal here.** (After all, we all have hot flashes.) I don't mind mistakes at all. I would rather have you try a new financial skill and make a mistake than be too afraid that you won't do it perfectly the first time.

At *Hot Flash Financial,* there are no bad mistakes. You can learn from every mistake while you get some practice doing these new things. Besides, I want to encourage you to find humor in mistakes, any mistake you make. Mistakes can be **hilarious** if you think about them. You can weave your mistakes into great stories and then get others to giggle or guffaw as you recount them.

> **Use laughter as a weapon.** *Make a mistake? No worries. Just giggle, snicker, or even cackle. That is the best way to reduce your stress and anxiety about these financial issues. Then take action.*

Okay, if you need another reason to begin this process, I will give you one.

If you take the *Hot Flash Financial* STEPS, you will **have less stress.** What I mean is that you will have

- **less money stress,**
- **more control** over your money and your life,
- and probably **more money!**

Remember, you *CANNOT put this off.* And if you don't listen, your hot flashes will remind you. **So every time you get a HOT FLASH, every time you feel that heat rising and you start to sweat, remember to**

- open this book,
- read a new chapter, and
- **take another** *Hot Flash Financial* **STEP toward greater financial security.**

Oh, and don't be too serious now. Ya gotta giggle a little. *And remember, don't try to be too perfect!*

IN A FLASH—A QUICK SUMMARY

So now you know what hot flashes are really for. They remind you to focus on your money and your future so you can increase your financial security. Because they nag you, you can't forget what they say and put things off anymore Ya gotta start now. So work with me so you can reach that really important goal—financial security. (And remember to laugh a little bit along the way!)

HOT FLASH QUIZ #1

1. What is your definition of a woman who is economically and/or financially secure?

a. Second wife of an old geezer.

b. Divorcee (who had a very good lawyer) when she divorced a very rich man.

c. Loyal, long-term wife of a man who has money (and who hasn't told her he likes younger women).

d. Woman who won the multistate lottery.

e. Woman who does not have to stress about money. In fact, she has a stash of cash in her own name and a lot of good friends. She shares good times with her friends, feels financially independent, and believes a laugh with friends is better than any $3,000 purse or $500 pair of shoes.

CHAPTER 2

Girl, Let's Talk

CHAPTER 2 GOALS:

Start by helping you understand the stress you may feel about money and the ways this tension can become an obstacle. Then think about the ways this fear restricts you from acting in your own self-interest. Encourage you to free yourself by learning some new ideas and skills so you can make better decisions and improve your finances.

Let's pick up the dialogue where we left off. Ready? Do you have some questions for me?

Well, I sure have some questions for **you.**

Question #1: What is keeping you from acting in your own self-interest?

There are times when you need to put yourself first, when your hot flashes start to tell you to focus on your financial security. This is one of those times.

So I ask you again: What is stopping you?

Question #2: Are you afraid that you just might not have enough money to pay for everything you need today ... and in your future?

Are you **too scared** even to look at your finances?

Are you **anxious** about opening this issue with your partner (if you have one)?

Can We *Talk*?

Scientists used to say that when people are afraid, they do one of two things: they *fight* what makes them scared, or they run away. The problem is that these old scientists were only talking about *men*.

When we women are afraid, we talk (or we run away). **So let's talk!**

Okay, if you feel funny about talking to a book, "think out loud" (when no one is listening). Or make a list.

List whatever obstacles make you nervous and stressed out about your money. You don't need to share them with anyone right now. Just write them down on a piece of paper.

Things that make me too afraid to even think about this money thing:

1. _____

_____

2. _____

_____

3. _____

_____

Okay, now take your first step toward financial security. Reduce your fears, anxieties, and tension. Take out a dart board and pin THIS LIST OF FEARS AND OBSTACLES to it. Then aim and fire!

Didn't that make you feel better?

Now, let's talk about that list. I am going to try to guess a few of the fears you jotted down. That way we can talk about the obstacles that keep you from acting in your own self-interest.

Guess #1: You are frightened about what you will find—or **NOT FIND!**

So you feel like putting this book down and running away.

Don't run away from *Hot Flash Financial.* A lot of us are anxious that we will not have enough money for our future.

But let me ask you this:

Question #3: How do you really know you won't have enough money? Did you ever sit down and make a list of *all the valuable things you own*?
No, not your Beanie Babies or old Barbies or even a dusty baseball card collection or your moldy Beatles records.

I am talking about the real valuable stuff:

- Your **savings accounts,** CDs (certificate of deposit), and bonds
- Your **retirement accounts,** all of them
- Your **house,** if you own one
- Your **rights to Social Security**

I want you to work with "what you actually have." Then you can follow the *Hot Flash Financial* STEPS to make yourself more secure.

Okay, can I get real here?

Remember, I am **not talking RICH** here. I am talking **comfortable,** *secure.* I am talking **realistic** about what is *possible.*

Once you know what you have as a base, you can make intelligent decisions about your next moves. How does that sound? Possible?

Let's continue to talk. Let's guess some more reasons for your concern.

Guess #2: Maybe you are afraid you **don't know enough.** You don't know where to start or what to do for yourself.

Let me be clear here: you are **NOT a bimbo!**

I know you *mean to* learn more about money and finance. You think that one day you might take a class or consult a website. You really do want to know more so you can make intelligent decisions about important money issues such as,

- when to take your last paycheck and
- when to start Social Security.

Maybe you need to make a careful decision about when and if you will sell your home and use that money to live on. It seems like a lot to think about so . . . you procrastinate.

But why wait?
You have already been waiting, oh, a decade . . . or three!
What has dawdling done to increase your knowledge, answer your most important questions, or improve your financial situation so far?

Remember, you have HOT FLASHES. And they tell you that **your life is changing.**

So change yourself as well.

Change what you know and *don't know* about your money and your future. Take my STEPS. Try some new things. You just tried one—throwing darts at your list of fears and obstacles. You released some tension and took action to overcome the obstacles holding you back. But there is more to do.

I want to use *Hot Flash Financial* to empower you by teaching you more. I still believe *knowledge is power*. So I spend a lot of pages explaining things to you. The more you read, the more you will feel informed. As your understanding increases, you will realize that you have more control. So I encourage you to take some more *Hot Flash Financial* STEPS so you can practice new skills. The more you try, the more capable and self-reliant you will become. You will feel better as you increase your control over your money and your future.

Hot Flash Financial *encourages you to*
- *take yourself seriously,*
- *act in your own self-interest,*
- *take steps to reduce your stress and reduce the risks you face,*
- *learn more about your money and finances, and*
- *feel more empowered.*

And don't forget to laugh. **Laugh** *a lot—it can really reduce your anxiety and, by doing so, help you improve your financial situation.*

Couples and Money

If you don't have a partner, you are done with most of this chapter. You don't have to worry about the following section. Skip it. Go to the page with Question #3. That's the question that asks you, "So what is better for you to do?"

Guess #3. This guess is for folks who are married or have a live-in partner: you are terrified that, if you start this process, you will open a Pandora's box with your partner.

So you **avoid the topic** at all costs. If you were to open the issue, there would be disagreements, finger pointing about past purchases, you name it ("you made me buy," "you wasted," etc.)

At *Hot Flash Financial* I understand this completely. I do NOT want this to happen to you. So let's think through the

possibilities and develop a strategy to approach this, one point at a time.

Marriages and other partnerships can be good, but there can be some challenges. And arguments. I understand that couples argue about money more than anything else—even sex.

So let's be smart here. Let's *not* open a Pandora's box.

If you decide to get serious about your money and your future, *develop a careful strategy to introduce this idea to your partner.*

In the process:
- Be extremely diplomatic and sensitive to your partner's feelings and perspective.
- Begin gently. You are not attempting to change the names on accounts or take his/her name off an account. Be clear that that is NOT YOUR OBJECTIVE.
- Make sure you are not *seen as* trying to take control from your partner. (And be clear that you do not suspect your partner is hiding something.)
- Explain that you really just want to learn more (not wrestle nor rumble).
- Start the conversation with a fact.
- If your partner is a man, explain to him that you are likely to outlive him because you are a woman. (This is especially true if he is older than you.) So you have to know something about the money you *both* have. That way you will be able to make good decisions about money and your future—***before you are "in crisis."*** This is a kind of *insurance* that costs nothing but patience. It *really pays off if your partner becomes disabled, unconscious, or terribly ill and/or you become a widow. You will know what to do.*

- Make clear that are on a "fact-finding mission" right now (at least until you finish this book). You want to clarify things for yourself. Please make sure your partner understands that.
- Tell your partner you want to collaborate. You want to review account statements and files together. Ask your partner to work with you to help you understand what you have and what has been done *so far*. You want to be able to find important account information for retirement and/or investment accounts that are held, maybe savings accounts or treasury bonds or CDs, insurance documents, deeds, titles, and so forth.
- Propose, if it seems politic, developing a twenty-first-century computer-based filing system that clarifies and organizes everything for you both. Once again, you can remind your partner that you are not taking over. You can work together to update and scan key information. Or just organize paper-based files in a neat, clear, and understandable system.

A few sins you should not commit:
- Do NOT ask why your partner did or did NOT do something. For example, do not be upset with your partner if s/he let an insurance policy lapse. (Flip to the pages of the Glossary to help you understand any word or concept that baffles you.)
- Do NOT blame your partner for or accuse him/her of some of the seven deadly sins, such as greed, waste, or gluttony. This is not part of the *Hot Flash Financial* program. Don't get angry. Do get the facts. Peacekeeping is essential. (You can pretend you are Secretary of State Hillary Clinton negotiating across the table with a sensitive person, like either the Iranian or North Korean president—you must proceed carefully.)

Question #4: So what is better for *you* to do?
  Be afraid?
  Be too scared?
  Ignore this?
  Continue to DO NOTHING?

It will cost you too much *if* you ignore these financial questions. Why? At one point you are likely to find yourself "in crisis" because of

- a serious illness,
- the loss of a job,
- the loss of a second income, or
- the loss of a partner.

And then what will you do?

You need to know more about *your* money, before that crisis comes. Many, many years before. If you know more, you will be able to act in an intelligent manner and make careful decisions at that time.

> *Money is like oxygen: you need both to live. If you don't know if you have the money to support yourself or where your money will come from, you will be gasping for breath.*

I have to say this again because it is so important (and so many people like to procrastinate and ignore this). If you do NOT DO something now, you are seriously INCREASING YOUR RISK that you will not have enough money

- because you will live a long time after your hot flashes start;
- because inflation will increasingly limit your ability to buy things, and you will not be able to afford life's little pleasures;
- because health care costs are rising faster than inflation, and you are likely to need more medical care as you age;
- because you can lose your job many years earlier than you planned—in fact before you get your financial act together; and
- because if you become a widow or get divorced, your income will drop.

So set aside your demons and work with me at *Hot Flash Financial.* I believe you are smart enough and capable enough to do this.

Trust me and *Hot Flash Financial.*

And most importantly, trust *yourself* to do this!

Question #5: What are you waiting for? Chin hairs to grow in?

IN A FLASH—A QUICK SUMMARY

*T*he goal of this chapter was to help you confront your own personal "demons," "obstacles," and "fears," then help you get beyond them by doing what we girls do best—talking.

If you smiled when you read our questions and laughed as you developed your own answers, you are ready to work with *Hot Flash Financial*. So read on. And start to take the STEPS I will give you.

Unless you want to wait for those chin hairs . . .

HOT FLASH QUIZ #2

What do you remember from chapter 2?

1. The chapter just encouraged you to focus on controlling your money and your future. What is your response? (You may select more than one.)

a. Forget that! I'm gonna go shopping.

b. Forget that! I will let my man take care of me.

c. I would rather see what Lady Gaga is wearing.

d. I had better read the next chapter and start to take steps to improve my life.

2. True or False:

____ I am older and wiser now.

____ I can act in my own financial self-interest.

____ If I don't act to improve my finances, no one else will do it for me.

____ I want to be a burden on my children.

3. When you decide to talk to your husband or partner about your financial security, what is the best diplomatic approach you can take?

a. Blame him for spending too much money.

b. Accuse him of not making enough money.

c. Tell him his system of organization sucks.

d. All of the above.

e. None of the above.

CHAPTER 3

It's Probably Not as Bad as You Think

CHAPTER 3 GOALS:

Encourage you to take some STEPS so you can relieve more of your stress. Persuade you to organize some of your most important papers. (Organizing your papers is a great way to organize your mind.) Then help you translate jargon and read a really important type of financial statement. By the time you finish these STEPS you will find out how much money you do have accumulated and what sources of income you can use, to increase your financial security. You will feel a lot better.

Okay, are you less worried about your money now that you finished the last chapter? Well, I am going to help reduce that stress a little more right now. How? I bet that you have already done some things to build financial security. Let's find out *what you have done right* so far.

Together we are going on a **treasure hunt** in your very own home. You won't need a map. You just need to look for clues, like stacks of those unopened envelopes mailed to you each month—you know, the ones from the banks and retirement account programs, the ones you have probably been ignoring for years *(tee hee)*.

You may have to do some archeology and dig down through layers of paper debris until you reach that gold.

Your Treasure

What is that gold? Your treasure is your pile of **assets.**

> *HOT FLASH TRANSLATION.* Assets *are resources that have real value (in money terms), like savings, retirement and investment accounts, and real estate. What is more, these are* **resources you *own* or *control***. *And you invest in them because you* **expect them to** *benefit you in the future*.

Ahhhh, that is the crucial bit of knowledge for you *Hot Flash Financial* Mamas who want to increase your financial security.

What kinds of benefits could your assets give you in the *future*?
• money to fund everything you need to pay for today and tomorrow
• a life of leisure and laughter with your best friends and the ones you love
• the rest of your life with no worries and low stress, with sun in the sky and a light wind blowing your hair
• a life in which you can do what you love, every day.

So let's find out what assets you have so far. They are your base, the foundation on which you will build a secure future.

Finding That Treasure

In the twenty-first century your treasure is held in your accounts at banks, or retirement programs, etc., not in a buried wooden trunk with an antique lock. These financial institutions have to report how much they have stored for you and what they do with your money—such as receive deposits, subtract withdrawals, or recognize a change in the dollar value of the assets held. Everything they do is summarized in *account statements*. Those are the pieces of paper that come in those big envelopes.

So here is your first *Hot Flash Financial* STEP.

STEP 1: Find your account statements for every account in your and your partner's name (if you have a partner).

Yep, locate them **all**. If you have a partner who has filed and organized this material, you are lucky. Now you are simply on a fact-finding mission, so all you need to do is understand the existing system of organization and then build on it.

If you are like most of us, however, and do not have a resident file slave, you have work to do. You may need to sit down and make a list of the accounts you remember having. Think of every savings and retirement account you have. And think of every one your partner may hold. Include all the CDs you and your partner might have, the US savings bonds you might have stored somewhere, and any investment accounts. Try to remember every institution or bank where you hold a CD and where you put those bonds. And try to remember every job you had and every job your partner ever had. Why? You and your partner may have opened a retirement account with that former employer. Also make sure you look for a retirement account with your present employer and your partner's employer. If you have any investment accounts, list them too, and look for the statements. Investment accounts can be held jointly.

Don't forget to list IRAs (Individual Retirement Accounts) in your name and in your partner's name. They can be Roth IRAs, SEP IRAs, or what are called rollover IRAs. (The last one is not really a technical name for a retirement account; you just hear about rollovers through advertising.) And if you or your partner have a pension, deferred compensation, or stock options, find the statements or reports for them.

Now that you have your list of accounts, hunt for each one. Remember, this is your first effort—you don't have to be perfect and find every account statement. It is good to try this out. Once you follow all the steps in this chapter you will understand their importance. So, the second time you compile your list of assets you can get more thorough and assemble a more complete set. It is a good idea to do this every year, perhaps in January, when every institution sends your year-end account statements. Right now, your job is to just "get the hang of this" and start to organize this important information.

Another hunting method is to use online access.

HOT FLASH TRANSLATION: Online access is when you can go online to gain access to all of your accounts through a financial institution's website. If you have not done this yet, now is a good time to start. And you can go green by downloading the statements and any other relevant information into digital files. You are ready for the future.

STEP 2: Start to get organized.

Once you have located these account statements or gone online to get them, you will need to develop some kind of order. You can use a traditional paper-based pile-and-file system; color code it and coordinate the colors to your heart's content. Or you can develop a computer-based system for organizing and storing your financial information. That lets you download information that is up to date while also reducing the paper clutter. In addition, you can store it efficiently because digital files take up much less room. But they still have to be organized.

At *Hot Flash Financial,* I suggest you make separate *piles* or maybe separate *files* for each of the five following statements and types of assets:

• savings accounts, CDs, and bonds, no matter what the institution

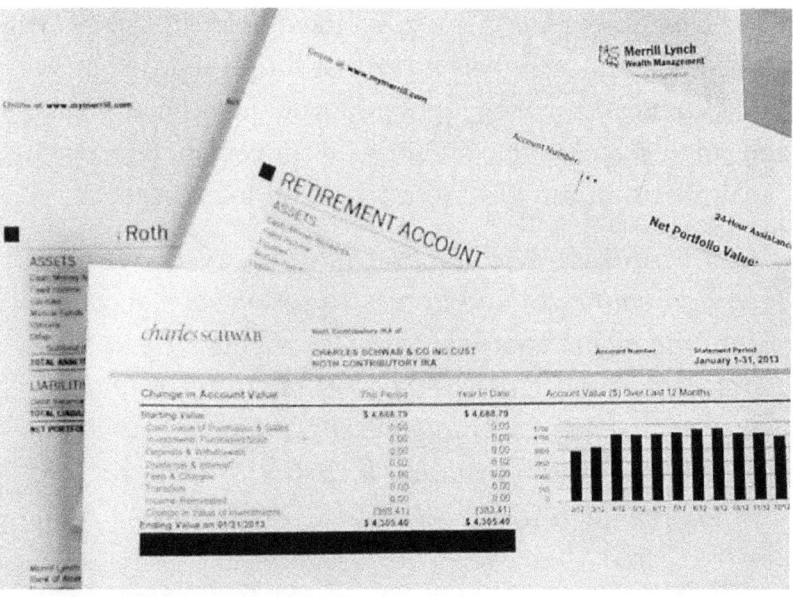

- retirement accounts held by employers (also called 401k, 403b, or 457 accounts)
- retirement accounts held as IRAs, whether traditional IRAs, Roth IRAs, SEP IRAs, simple IRAs, and so forth
- pensions and/or annuities, if you have them
- deferred compensation and/or stock options, if you have them

> *Organizing your papers becomes a great start to organizing your mind.*

Ready for the next step? It will really increase your knowledge and give you a greater sense of power over your financial future.

STEP 3: Read these statements, and then create a list of *your* assets.

Now that you have all your account statements together, **read them.** Count your gold.

I am going to teach you this new reading skill. We will start off easy: begin with the account types that are probably familiar to you, such as your savings accounts, CDs, and so forth. After you master reading them, review the other types of statements, the ones that tell you what assets you hold in your retirement accounts and others.

Eyeball a few of these statements to "get the hang of" reading them. Each institution may print the dates or account numbers in different places. That should not hold you back; just get to know your way around these statements. This is a great *Hot Flash Financial* skill to master.

> *Remember, each account statement lists*
> - *the name of the institution that holds the account,*
> - *the name of the person who **owns** the account,*
> - *the account type (IRA, savings, etc.),*
> - *the account number, and*
> - *the amount of money and total amount (or balance) held in that account on a specific day of the year.*

Now let's work together to do the most important thing in this chapter: find out exactly how much money you have—and where it is stashed.

Fill out the LIST OF ASSETS we provide. Or, even better, become familiar with computer programs that will do a lot of the calculating work for you, like an Excel spreadsheet. Learning this type of software will be very helpful—you get a "math slave." No need for a calculator. All you have to do is type in a few numbers on the spreadsheet and maybe key in a few functions, like ADD. And if you use Excel, you can download the *Hot Flash Financial* List of Assets from our website, www.hotflashfinancial.com. (Go to the TOOLS tab on the nav bar. Use the drop-down menu to access the List of Assets. See our Resources List to find out how to do this. Once you enter the numbers, they will add up automatically for you.)

If you are creating your own LIST OF ASSETS or want to figure out how *Hot Flash Financial* organized the List of Assets, use the table below. Start with Column 1 on the left.

Column 1. Name of account owner (this is you, your partner, or possibly a child).

LIST OF ASSETS

Name of owner and account number	Account type (IRA, etc.) and institution name	Dollar amount	Statement date
		$	
		$	
		$	
		$	
		$	
		$	
		$	
		GRAND TOTAL $	

Column 2. Account type (IRA, etc.) and institution that holds it. In this column make sure you write down and distinguish the *type of account,* such as savings account or retirement account, from the institution that holds it (e.g., Fidelity or Merrill Lynch, Morgan Stanley, or TD Ameritrade, etc.)

Column 3. Write in the total dollar amount, or balance, reported to be in that account in dollars on the date of the statement.

Column 4. Date for the statement for which you have the dollar figure. The dollar figures will change depending on the date the statement was written. (Make sure you are not listing account balances for 2003 in one account and for 2012 in another.) The best way to do this is to try to use the dollar figures for the most recent statement and/or statements issued on the same date, such as the last day of the last month. Or you can decide to restrict your list to statements for December 31 of last year. This is especially easy if you access your statements online. You can usually pull up each statement for a specific date. You generally use a drop-down menu or other method specific to that bank.

The structure for your List of Assets, organized into a neat table, is on the next page.

Okay, remember when I asked you to put your statements in piles, by account type, in STEP 2? Now take your first *pile* (or *file*) and enter the information for each of the four columns. That will give you a list of *all* of your savings accounts, CDs, and bonds. Then reach for the next pile (or file) and enter the information for all the retirement accounts held at work. Finally, fill in the information for all of the IRA accounts, including deferred comp, annuities, and stock options, if you or your partner have access to them.

Great job. You have mastered a really important skill: you can read and understand account statements. And you can translate the jargon and organize the information into a readable format. You now have a summary of the most important assets you have.

BRAVA!

STEP 4: Add up the dollar amounts at the bottom of the dollar column.

Now it's time to add up the value of your assets to find your **GRAND TOTAL.** Use your calculator or, if you used our *Hot Flash Financial* Excel spreadsheet, your math slave has added this for you.

Okay, my *Hot Flash Financial* Mama, you know what you have done right so far! **YOU HAVE MONEY,** or, more correctly, you have created **a LIST OF YOUR ASSETS.**

To paraphrase Austin Powers: "Yeah, baby, yeah. You have assets!"

You now know what resources you and your partner own and control. **The GRAND TOTAL is your foundation, the base upon which you can build a secure future for the twenty or thirty-plus years after your hot flashes start.**

Take a deep breath. And kiss your list, if you want.

STEP 5: Add in the value of your home.

Your home is also an asset, as is any other real estate you might have. So what dollar figure do we write in for your home and real estate? This is a little tricky.

You have to work with the dollar value of your home as if it were sold *today*. True, the value probably dropped. But don't worry about that: you are not selling it today. Just be truthful in your estimate. Go to www.trulia.com or perhaps redfin.com to get an *estimate* of the value of your house in today.

A Short Hot Flash Financial Digression

Many of you are worried about the drop in the market value of your home since 2007. And there is a good reason you are concerned.

For many of you, your home is your biggest ASSET.

But I am talking about finances and assets here. And I am talking about future benefits. So think carefully here. Your home is an asset that is very likely to benefit you many years into the future—when you sell it. So you only need to worry about "the market value" or price of your house *when* you put it on the market and actually sell it. So don't worry about the drop in value today.

Your home is a very valuable resource. If you own a home, you have quite a few options. You can draw on this resource in a variety of ways during the twenty or thirty-plus years *after your hot flashes begin.*

In addition to living in your home, you can also

- rent it,
- rent some rooms,
- take out a home equity line of credit or perhaps a reverse mortgage, and, finally,
- sell it.

When you sell it, you can keep the *equity* and use it to pay for everything you need, or a portion of what you need, in the future.

> *HOT FLASH TRANSLATION:* Equity *is the amount of money that you can "put in your pocket" after you subtract the money you still owe on your mortgage. Remember, when you sell your home, the bank will take all the money that you still owe on your mortgage. You walk away with the remaining amount, called the equity.*

The amount of equity in your home increases as you pay down your mortgage loan. It also increases as the housing market goes up over time. Thus, the equity dollar figure, like the balances in your savings and other accounts, changes over time.

To find the equity you have to do a little subtraction. Here's a simple example. Let's say you could sell your house for

$150,000, but you still have a mortgage of $100,000. Subtract the mortgage balance ($100,000) from the amount you could get from the sale ($150,000). The equity you have in your house today is whatever would be left over from the sale *after the mortgage is paid.* In our example it is $50,000.

Okay, let's find out how much equity you have in your home today. After you find the estimated selling price of your home on www.trulia.com or another reliable website, find your mortgage statement. Look for the total dollar amount *or balance remaining to be paid on your mortgage.* Do the subtraction.

If you need a formula, here is the way you calculate it:

Take your current ESTIMATED (trulia.com) VALUE OF YOUR HOME, then subtract the TOTAL BALANCE REMAINING on your MORTGAGE today.

Voila! That equals the EQUITY you have IN YOUR HOME at this point in time.

Okay, now to complete your List of Assets, add in the equity value of your home for this specific time period.

STEP 6: Recalculate the grand total of your assets by adding in the amount of equity you hold.

Write that Grand Total amount in HUGE NUMBERS. You will need to remember this GRAND TOTAL as you think about your future and your financial security. That GRAND TOTAL is your foundation for paying your bills each and every month in the future.

Wait, there is more money you can use to be financially secure.

If you are or were employed (and/or your partner is or was employed), you have a right to benefits from Social Security. That US government program *will provide money for you to live on each month based on your employment record and/or the employment of your legal spouse.* So if you have not been employed but are married to someone who is or was employed (or divorced from someone employed yet married for at least ten years), you are also eligible to receive Social Security through your spouse.

So the next bit of knowledge you need is important.

STEP 7: Find out how Social Security will help you. (Yes, it is funded until 2036 at the time of this writing.)

Look through your files or go online for the information from the Social Security Administration. The paper document is called "Your Social Security Statement." The web page is called ESTIMATED BENEFITS.

> *HOT FLASH TRANSLATION:* Social Security *provides an estimate of the benefits you are eligible to receive after you reach a specific age and apply for benefits. You are likely to be amazed at what you can receive from the government. Your Social Security benefit is likely to become a very important percentage of your future income. More good news, Social Security benefits will go up with inflation. So take a careful look at this estimate. You need to know what Social Security makes available to you so that you can make good decisions about your future income and security.*

• If you decide to rely on the older printed "Your Social Security Statement," open it to page 2. On the top of that page you will see a section called *Your Estimated Benefits*. Focus on that part. Look below that to the information on Retirement.

• Look across the top of page 2 to the right where you see dollar figures. Begin looking down the page at the *third dollar amount*. It says, on the left, "if you continue working until . . . age 70, your payment (each month) would be about $X,XXX."

• Focus on the dollar amount *for age seventy*. That is the largest dollar amount you are likely to receive as monthly income from Social Security. To get that amount each month, you have to delay starting your Social Security benefits until age seventy. (Think about developing a strategy for your income until then.)

- There is another dollar figure above it. That is the estimate of the dollar amount you will get if you work until you reach retirement age or wait to start your benefits until that age. For most Boomers that is age sixty-six. That monthly amount $X,XXX is less than the amount you would receive if you wait to start benefits until age seventy. But it is still a good base.
- Of course, you can start your Social Security benefits at age sixty-two. That amount will be even smaller than the amount you would receive if you waited to start your benefits at age sixty-six, and it will be a lot less than the amount you would receive if you wait until age seventy.
- If you go online, you can get the latest estimate of your benefits. And you can open your own Social Security Account. So go online to the protected government site www.socialsecurity.gov. You will have to create a new, very secure username and password to prevent identity thieves from stealing your benefits and possibly your identity. So expect to answer a lot of questions that will verify your identity. And do not enter any of them unless you see the web address that shows you are on the secure social security site—**Https://secure.ssa.gov/RIR/. . .** Answer questions, and get creative with passwords. You will have to mix capital letters, lower case letters, numbers, and symbols. Get creative. Rather than **toocutecat**, try **Cat2Cute*** or **caT2cuTe!** Or **2cuTe!cAT**. You can do it.

When you open your very own, personal account, click on the tab that says MY HOME. Then look at the bar below it and find ESTIMATED Benefits. Click on that.

Go right to the section that reads **Retirement.**

Now here is the important part. Just as I suggested above, follow these steps in order.

- **First Step.** Look below that Retirement bar to the **SECOND LINE, which says At age 70:**
- **Second Step.** Read the dollar amount that you are estimated to receive from social security **at age 70. What is that figure?** $X,XXX? Focus on that dollar amount. It is likely to be the largest monthly benefit that Social Security will send you. As said earlier, to get that larger amount, you will have to delay starting your benefits until you reach age 70. (Think of a strategy that will help you do that. Work longer?)
- **Third step.** Look above that to the first line, that says **At full retirement age (66)**
- **Fourth Step.** What is that dollar amount that you are estimated to receive from Social Security **at age 66**? $XXX? That is the amount you are likely to receive if you stop working at age 66 and start your benefits. This is likely to be a smaller than the amount you would receive it you decide to delay the start of your benefits. It still can become an important source of income for you.
- **Fifth Step.** And now, look at the amount you would receive at age 62 or your current age. What is that dollar figure? $XXX. It is probably the smaller than the monthly payment you would receive it you waited until you were 66, and even smaller than the benefits you would receive age at age 70.

So you just learned some really important things. **You have a right to an income stream** from Social Security. And **you have the power to decide how much money,** or which dollar amount you are likely to receive. You just have to decide *when* **you will start your benefits.**

> *One of the most important decisions you will make about your future income will be choosing the year you want to start your Social Security benefits.*

Since Social Security benefits are probably the only income that you will receive that will go up with inflation your decision is very, very important So if you can wait until you are seventy to start your benefits, an inflation increase of 2 percent of your benefits (starting at age seventy) will be a lot more dollars than 2 percent of the benefit you would receive if you started early, such as at age sixty-two. I repeat: **your decision about the timing of your first benefit will have a huge impact on the amount of money you receive each month for the rest of your life.**

Oh, and don't forget the US government helps pay for your medical care—that is, if you apply for Medicare "on time": at least three months before you turn sixty-five. There are some more decisions that you will need to make about Medicare. For instance, you may decide you want to buy a supplemental plan to help you pay for your medical expenses in the future.

Whatever you decide with respect to supplemental insurance, Medicare can help you cover your bills as you age and your medical costs rise.

You can start to breathe a sigh of relief, right?

Okay, financial security is not looking so impossible now that you have learned some new concepts, practiced some new skills, and totaled your assets. Way to go, girl!

> *Don't you feel better?*
> *Less stressed?*
> *More secure?*

Congratulations! You overcame inertia. The obstacle of anxiety did not stop you. You have decreased your RISKS.
Why not celebrate?

IN A FLASH—A QUICK SUMMARY

You have learned a lot in this chapter. First, you picked up key concepts, like assets and equity. And you began to use them to organize your thoughts about your money and your future. Next, you took some important steps to organize your financial life. You located your account statements read them, then compiled your own List of Assets. Perhaps the most important step you took was adding up your Grand Total. Now you know what you have done right so far. Congratulations!

HOT FLASH QUIZ #3

1. What are assets?

a. Diamonds. Isn't that what Marilyn Monroe said? She said you have to "spend money to make money." So she bought herself diamonds. Then she sang a song about diamonds being "a girl's best friend." Are they really scarce?

b. Beanie babies. No wait. They *were supposed to be* assets.

c. Hummels. (You know, those figurines that break. And today they aren't worth $50, because so many were manufactured.)

d. All of the above.

e. None of the above.

2. True or False:

____ My system for organizing my finances looks like the floor of my teenager's room.

CHAPTER 4

Are There "Unsightly" Wrinkles in Your Financial Future?

CHAPTER 4 GOALS:

• Help you understand what you can change and how you can start to improve your financial security.
• Encourage you to start to build a larger pile of money for yourself so you can reduce those financial "wrinkles."

I am going to try to get fancy here—even poetic. Yes, you can snicker at my feeble attempts to be expressive and even lyrical when I use a metaphor to talk about your financial future. Go ahead and chuckle. As I've said, laughing is important.

Ready? When you compiled your List of Assets, you actually started to look into your "financial mirror." What did you

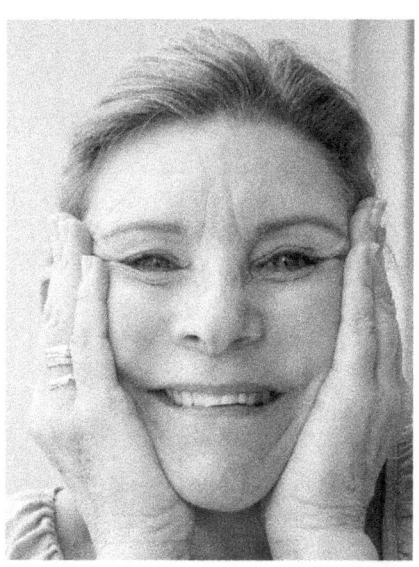

see? Did you have some financial blemishes? Maybe some liver spots, sagging skin under the chin, frown lines, forehead wrinkles, eye wrinkles . . .

Let's face it: many of us have "wrinkles" in our finances.

So, ask yourself: What is the **biggest, ugliest,** most **"unsightly wrinkle"** that **you have in your financial future?**

Answer: If you are like most people in America today, you have a huge wrinkle in your financial future. That is, you don't have enough money in savings—yet.

You do NOT have a **HOT FLASH STASH OF CASH.**

What is this "stash"?

A HOT FLASH STASH OF CASH is money in *an account, or set of accounts,* such as a savings account, CD, investment account, or retirement account that has *your name on it.* You own it. Yes, it is an asset.

What makes it a **Hot Flash Stash of Cash**?

In your mind you keep these assets *separate from the money you use every day.* In other words, you think of these assets, you "frame them" as separate and, therefore, *untouchable, except for your future* benefit.

So when you think of this money, you are clear about its future *benefit, in that it* will *fund your future*—so **you will have** *a future of financial security.*

Your Hot Flash Stash of Cash might not be big now, but it can and *will become a significant amount.* At *Hot Flash Financial,* I encourage you to **take STEPS to increase the size of your Hot Flash Stash of Cash—and reduce the wrinkles in your financial future.**

Don't get intimidated. Remember, the *Hot Flash Financial* objective is to have enough money to pay for everything you need so you will be independent and maintain your dignity. I want you to build your Stash over time s**o you will have a lovely,** *comfortable* **cushion of money.**

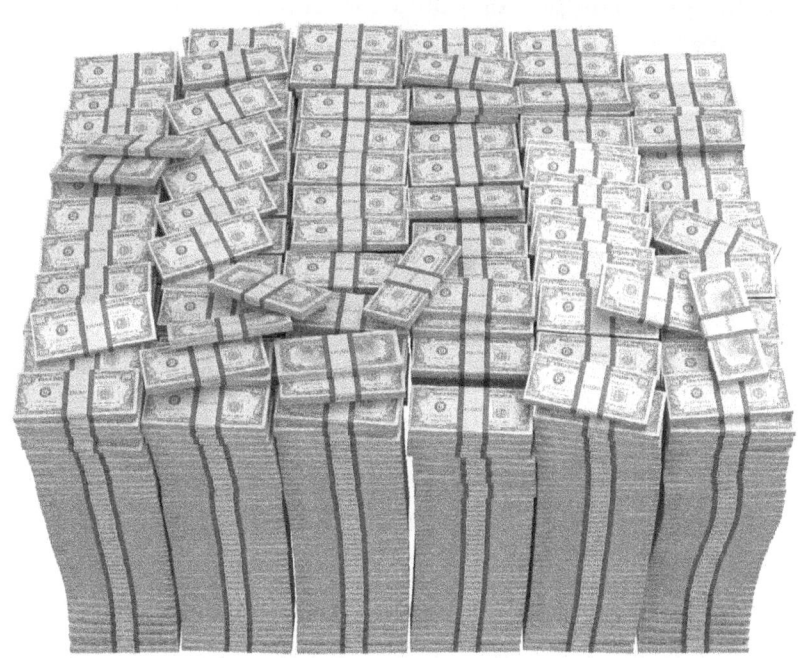

So start thinking while you are stuck in a boring meeting or someplace where your mind can be doing something else. Ask yourself:

- What am I going to do about this financial "wrinkle"?
- How am I going to build my own personal Hot Flash Stash of Cash?

In fact, this can be what you ask yourself **each time you get a HOT FLASH for the next year.** Finding the answer or set of answers will take a lot of thought.

> *Every time you get a hot flash, let it remind you of the important work you have to do: reduce the wrinkles in your financial future. Figure out how you are going to build your Hot Flash Stash of Cash.* **Hot Flash Financial** *is going to give you a brilliant way to start.*

STEP 8: Begin by depositing a portion of each paycheck *into your own HOT FLASH STASH every time you get paid.*

Even if you do not work, take a percentage of your partner's income (with her/his permission) and deposit it **into your STASH.**

It doesn't take much effort. But it is a "Best Practice." In the twenty-first century all you have to do is set up an **automatic deposit** into your very own **Hot Flash Stash of Cash.**

Okay, I know what you are thinking: you want to wait until you make more money before you start depositing money from your paycheck.

But you did that already.

Did waiting to make more money actually work?

How about starting **NOW?!**

There are *two* really good reasons to start to put money into your account NOW:

1. Depositing (even) small regular amounts **add up** to big savings *over time.* (But—*teehee*—"small" does not mean a few cents.)

Doing this is also called "investing in yourself."

Investing is not really that strange to us girls. But we tend to limit ourselves to investing in relationships . . . with friends, family, and, especially, loved ones. We offer small yet meaningful "deposits"—a kind word, a little support—each day, week, and year to get a far bigger return in the future. In effect, we build secure relationships over time, compounding on a regular basis the positive impact of small contributions of kindness.

Do the same thing with your money! Add a contribution from each paycheck over time. You will get a bigger and sweeter return in your financial future.

2. You can get the *"miracle of compounding"* to work wonders on the size of your Hot Flash Stash of Cash.

You are probably saying, "Wait! She is talking miracles here? Hold it!"

Let *Hot Flash Financial* explain this miracle. It uses math, just as your computer uses math to create e-mail, e-vites, and online calculators.

Now don't run away screaming 'cause I said "math." Just remember that compound interest makes your dollar amount **grow really fast,** or exponentially. That means that your money grows more rapidly than if you just added $200 each month to a pile of money under your mattress.

Trust me. The miracle of compounding interest works. Or go one better. Stick with me. Follow my explanation of the way this miracle of exponential growth can work for you.

Yes, there is math. But you can use a computer calculator to make it easy. That way, if you type in a few numbers on a website, you can see how this miracle benefits you. By the end of this section you will increase your knowledge about the secrets of finance—you can get this miracle to work for you, even while you sleep.

Go online and play with the compound interest calculators. Try www.thecalculatorsite.com. Click on the compound interest calculator.

In the Base amount slot, type in the total amount you have in your retirement account (for example, I will pretend you have $67,000 in your retirement account). So type in 67000. This calculator does not want the dollar sign or the comma in there.

Below that there is a slot for Annual interest rate. Type in

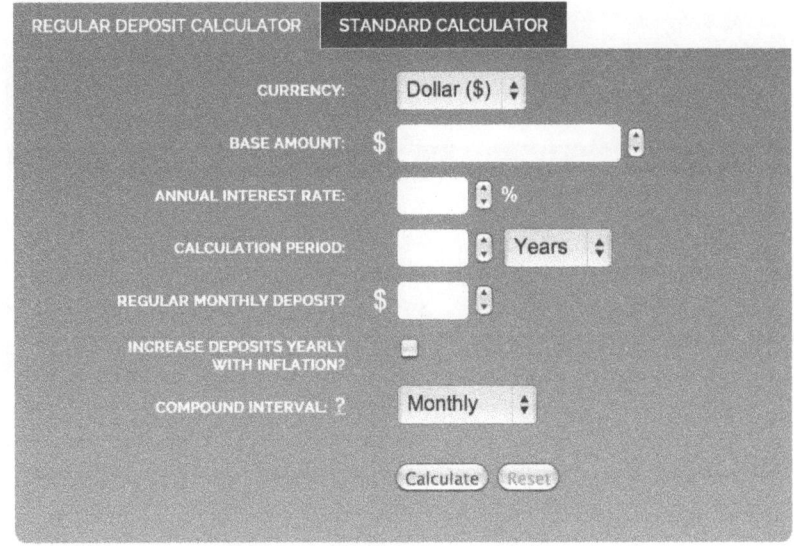

4. Why 4? Interest rates are abnormally low right now (2013). So use a slightly higher rate. That rate is a compromise between the average rate of long-term return in the stock market (7 percent) and a lower rate of return in a savings account or a safe Treasury bond today, in 2013.

Next to the CALCULATION PERIOD OR YEARS slot, type 20.

Okay, now focus on the impact of regular monthly deposits. In the slot titled Regular monthly deposit, type in 200. That is $200 per month, or $50 per week, taken from your paycheck and deposited in an account. If you get paid twice a month, it is $100 every paycheck.

Now let the computer do the math—click on the Calculate button.

Look at how your money will grow ... exponentially! You only deposit the same $200 a month, or $2,400 per year (see column 2, Year Deposits). That means you took only $48,000 over twenty years. But after compound interest works its

CALCULATION RESULTS	GRAPHS OF RESULTS				
(interest compounded **monthly** - added at the end of each month)					
Year	Year Deposits	Year Interest	Total Deposits	Total Interest	Balance
1	$ 2,400.00	$ 2,782.32	$ 69,400.00	$ 2,782.32	$ 72,182.32
2	$ 2,400.00	$ 2,993.46	$ 71,800.00	$ 5,775.78	$ 77,575.78
3	$ 2,400.00	$ 3,213.20	$ 74,200.00	$ 8,988.98	$ 83,188.98
4	$ 2,400.00	$ 3,441.89	$ 76,600.00	$ 12,430.87	$ 89,030.87
5	$ 2,400.00	$ 3,679.90	$ 79,000.00	$ 16,110.77	$ 95,110.77
6	$ 2,400.00	$ 3,927.60	$ 81,400.00	$ 20,038.37	$ 101,438.37
7	$ 2,400.00	$ 4,185.40	$ 83,800.00	$ 24,223.76	$ 108,023.76
8	$ 2,400.00	$ 4,453.70	$ 86,200.00	$ 28,677.46	$ 114,877.46
9	$ 2,400.00	$ 4,732.93	$ 88,600.00	$ 33,410.38	$ 122,010.38
10	$ 2,400.00	$ 5,023.53	$ 91,000.00	$ 38,433.92	$ 129,433.92
11	$ 2,400.00	$ 5,325.98	$ 93,400.00	$ 43,759.90	$ 137,159.90
12	$ 2,400.00	$ 5,640.75	$ 95,800.00	$ 49,400.64	$ 145,200.64
13	$ 2,400.00	$ 5,968.34	$ 98,200.00	$ 55,368.98	$ 153,568.98
14	$ 2,400.00	$ 6,309.28	$ 100,600.00	$ 61,678.26	$ 162,278.26
15	$ 2,400.00	$ 6,664.11	$ 103,000.00	$ 68,342.37	$ 171,342.37
16	$ 2,400.00	$ 7,033.39	$ 105,400.00	$ 75,375.76	$ 180,775.76
17	$ 2,400.00	$ 7,417.72	$ 107,800.00	$ 82,793.48	$ 190,593.48
18	$ 2,400.00	$ 7,817.71	$ 110,200.00	$ 90,611.20	$ 200,811.20
19	$ 2,400.00	$ 8,234.00	$ 112,600.00	$ 98,845.20	$ 211,445.20
20	$ 2,400.00	$ 8,667.24	$ 115,000.00	$ 107,512.44	$ 222,512.44

magic over those twenty years, you will have $222,512 as the total in your retirement account (see column 6, Balance, right there at the bottom). NICE!

The miracle occurs when your interest compounds. This means you will earn interest on your earned interest. So that will multiply to $107,512 (see the bottom of column 5, Total Interest). In other words, **compounding interest gives you much more money than the** puny **$200 per month you deposited.** Let me say that again: you only took $48,000 from your paycheck over twenty years, and **you compounded an** additional **$107,512. So the total amount of money in your name grew miraculously—or exponentially—to $222,512.**

Now play a bit so you can see how well this magic works. On the computer screen, click on the AMEND INFORMATION in the blue button below. Keep your $200 a month contribution the same. But now bump up the ANNUAL INTEREST RATE to 7 percent. This interest rate is closer to the *average annual rate of return for stocks over a long period of time, like twenty years (even including big drops in the stock market)*.

During the same twenty-year period your Total Balance will increase to **$375,388**. Once again you only deposited $200 per month, $2,400 per year, and $48,000 in total. But that relatively small deposit grew by $260,388 because the interest compounded.

> *You can grow your deposits into a WHOPPING HOT FLASH STASH OF CASH. That's because of the "miracle of compound interest" acting on the money you accumulated plus continuing, regular deposits. Now you can see why you should build a Hot Flash Stash of Cash over time: it will greatly increase your financial security.*

Okay, I hope I just got your jaw to drop. Yes, compound interest is a miracle that you can believe in. So why not take advantage of it today?

DON'T WAIT!

Remember: compounding interest works miracles for you most effectively over a *long* period of time. Now, if you have just started your hot flashes, you probably have thirty-plus years to plan for. Maybe you have forty-plus years after the heat rises and the sweat starts pouring out. Think about the financial magic you could create if you deposit $200 per month *and* earn compound interest—starting today. Think of how BIG your HOT FLASH STASH OF CASH could become in twenty or even thirty years!

Well, you might say, I don't have any extra cash to deposit each month!

I will tell you that that is what HOT FLASH FINANCES IS ALL ABOUT. **I want you to find money in your paycheck and control it**—so you can control your future. Here are a few tricks.

1. Every time you get a Hot Flash, put some more money in YOUR OWN NAME in your Hot Flash Stash of Cash. Make it $20 or $50 each time. It can add up to $200+ in a month.

How? Drink the coffee at work rather than buying fancy coffee that is $3 or $4 per drink. Reduce the number of times per month that you buy food in restaurants for yourself and your family. (There are so many tricks. I would need to write a whole book . . . so I will write one in the future.)

2. If you get a hot flash near a cash register, think twice about spending money. After all, you can have that money IN YOUR NAME. Why not deposit that money in your Hot Flash Stash that you did not give to the cashier?

3. If you get a hot flash when your teenager is begging for some more money, stand strong. Say, "No."

4. If you get a hot flash when your adult child is asking for another loan that s/he will not repay, stand strong. Say, "No."

Here are some additional ideas. They will help you take larger stashes of money to invest in yourself. (I am getting a bit more serious here, so my ideas are phrased in a more serious manner.)

5. Every time you (or your partner) receive a **raise,** put that extra money in your Hot Flash Stash and try to live within the amount of cash you *used to* take home.

6. Every time you (or your partner) are rewarded with a **bonus,** put that money in your Hot Flash Stash and try to keep your expenses low, just as they were before you had the bonus.

7. When you get your **tax refund check,** put that money in your Hot Flash Stash of Cash.

> *These are just a few ideas. You can develop your own answers. If you get some other good ideas, send them to me at Hotflashfinances@gmail.com. I will post your best ideas on www.hotflashfinancial.com.*

Okay, *Hot Flash Financial* has shown you how to think about your money and your future in a new, smarter way. I want you to start to develop a really important skill: managing your money. You do that by depositing a portion of your paychecks into your Stash. You get the benefit of the miracle of compounding interest. This way, you build your own big, wonderful, juicy, Zaftig, ginormous HOT FLASH STASH OF CASH to increase your financial security.

Don't delay! ACT today! (Just like they say on those commercials).

IN A FLASH—A QUICK SUMMARY

I told you that you have a "wrinkle" in your financial future, just like most Americans. Then I shared the *Hot Flash Financial* "beauty secret" with you: deposit a nice chunk of change into your Stash every paycheck. And take advantage of the miracle of compound interest to build a nice big Hot Flash Stash of Cash.

Fight that unsightly wrinkle! There are no creams, no painful injections, no overly bright lasers—just build a nice, large, comfy cushion of cash for your future. A big Hot Flash Stash of Cash is "clinically proven" to have a positive impact on your financial security for the rest of your life.

HOT FLASH QUIZ #4

Short Answers:

1. What kind of Stash did we talk about in chapter 4?

2. Why would we want that Stash to have your name on it?

Essay Questions:

1. How can you increase the size of your Stash? Can you grow your own? How?

2. Consider this: you are trying to resolve the problem of having an "unsightly wrinkle." You have two options.

Option 1: Every two months buy $100 worth of wrinkle cream (or $600 per year). Slather it on every day.

Option 2: Every two months deposit $100 in your Hot Flash Stash of Cash ($600 per year).

After ten years which use of your hard-earned $100 will have the longest-lasting impact on your "wrinkles"? Is it:

a. spending $6,000 on wrinkle cream? When you look in the mirror—one of those magnifying ones—will they really be gone?

b. investing $6,000 in your financial security? Look in your Hot Flash Stash of Cash. Doesn't that look better?

CHAPTER 5

Here's a Face Lift (For Your Finances)

CHAPTER 5 GOALS:

• *Tell you what types of accounts are best for building your Hot Flash Stash.*
• *Encourage you to use accounts that give you tax breaks at the same time that they help you build your Hot Flash Stash of Cash.*
• *Find more ways to reduce the "wrinkles" in your financial security by clarifying the steps you can take to have the biggest "wrinkle reduction" impact.*

After reading the last chapter you probably want to start building your Hot Flash Stash. But you might want to ask a really good question first: Where is the best place to stash your Hot Flash Cash?

Do **NOT** stash your cash HERE, under your mattress.

If you want to apply our miracle cure to reduce your "financial wrinkles," you have to deposit your first set of paycheck dollars into an account that compounds your returns.

Hot Flash Financial wants you to start that process using a specific type of account, one that not only offers compounding interest over a long period of time but also a tax break.

Really? Isn't that too good to be true?

Nope.

Ready for some important knowledge that will help you build a more secure future? The most advantageous type of account for you to use to build your Hot Flash Stash of Cash is a retirement account.

Why?

A retirement account is
- neatly labeled,
- *separated from the accounts* you use for daily spending,
- *set aside for your future,*
- builds your total *Stash over time* with each deposit, as it compounds and
- gives you an *excellent tax break too.*

There is a lot to explain here. So stick with me.

First, there are retirement accounts that an employer provides—generally called 401(k)s, 403(b)s, 457(b)s, or defined contribution plans. These accounts offer the most tax benefits. Then there are retirement accounts called IRAs (Individual Retirement Accounts).

This is important for you to know: even if you don't work and your marital partner does, you can have an IRA, called a *spousal IRA.* That way you have your own, legal, separate account set aside for your future.

So let's get started by explaining why this type of account should be the *first* (but not necessarily the only) place for you to *Stash your Hot Flash Cash.*

Retirement Accounts at Work: 401(k), 403(b), or 457(b), and Others Like Them

Retirement accounts offered by your employer give you the chance to easily and automatically Stash **good amounts of money AND reduce your taxes.** What is more, you might be able to increase the size of the monthly deposits in your retirement account if your company **offers you a "matching contribution."** Financial advisers like to remind you that a "match" is "free" money, which I'll talk about shortly. In addition, there are special benefits for us women who are fifty and older:

- **Tax breaks—they aren't just for the rich . . . here's one for you!** If you do deposit money from your paycheck into your retirement account at work, you get two big TAX BREAKS. First, you do not get taxed on the dollars you deposit into your retirement account at work! Yup, **your income taxes will drop.** So if you direct your company to send $1,000 of your paycheck into your retirement account, *you not only get that money deposited into an account with your name,* but you also get that same amount, that $1,000, *subtracted from the total amount of money the IRS* says it can *tax.* (I will use some IRS tax-speak here. It is called a **pre-tax amount.** It is the amount the company takes from your pay—and gives to you—even before they take out your taxes to pay Uncle Sam. If it is $1,000, then you reduce your taxable income by $1,000 for that pay period.)

    Let's get you an even bigger tax break. If you decide to deposit $10,000 this coming year into your retirement account, then you reduce your taxable income by $10,000! Remember you also get to deposit that money into an account in your name.

- In 2013 the IRS lets you deposit up to $17,500 per year, pre-tax, to your retirement account. This means that you can decrease your taxable income by up to $17,500!

    For many of you, depositing $17,500 may sound like a lot of money to take out of your wallet and put into your Hot Flash Stash of Cash. But let me just talk about it as a goal. For some of you it may be more possible to do if you think about this amount in smaller chunks.

Look at that amount every week for fifty-two weeks. To reach that target you would have to take something like $337 a week and give to yourself and your Stash. Now, you don't have to start taking $337 out of your weekly paycheck tomorrow, but you could work toward that larger target amount. (More on that later in this chapter.)

This type of tax break, depositing all that money into an account with your name on it, may seem like getting your cake and eating it too.

- **Get the cake**—You get your employer to deposit *your income* into an account with *your name* on it! You give yourself a gift at the same time as you get to build a nice Hot Flash Stash of Cash.
- **Eat the cake**—And you don't pay taxes on that income this year! (Or as the IRS says, **effectively pay less in taxes on your income** *now*.)

You know what else? During the years when you are contributing to your retirement account and building a nice-sized Stash, you are **NOT TAXED on the gain or compound interest** that you earn inside that account. Nice, huh? No tax on this Stash while it is growing inside your account.

Special Benefit for Hot Flash Mamas—the Catch-up Contribution. Many Americans are saving for their future. But as I mentioned, they have an *unsightly wrinkle*: They are a little behind in their saving. Their retirement accounts are kinda small.

So there has been a rule change that allows folks, like us Hot Flash Mamas who are **fifty years old or older**, to contribute more to our retirement accounts each year. The IRS says that we can try to catch up by depositing as much as an additional $5,500 in 2013. This is called—you guessed it—a Catch-Up Contribution.

(Maybe old Uncle Sam feels something for us mature Hot Flash Mamas.)

Can I break this down a bit into more manageable amounts? Over a year that becomes just about $105 per week taken out of your taxable income—not bad.

> *When you think about building your own Hot Flash Stashes of Cash, put your first Stash dollars in your retirement account at work. You get the most bang for your taxable buck by taking this STEP.*

Finally, there is one more advantage to building your Hot Flash Stash of Cash in your retirement account at work:

Free Money. Some employers will deposit money into your retirement account—the one with your name on it—if you contribute to it too. This benefit is called a **Corporate Match** or **Matching Contribution**. If your employer offers it, your company will add more money to your retirement Stash of Cash, up to 3 percent of your total yearly salary. What that means is you get paid 3 percent more without even asking for a raise. But you only get a matching contribution *if* you automatically deposit a portion of your paycheck into your Retirement Stash of Cash. Because it is extra money—more than your wages—many of us call that "free money." See if your employer offers this extra perk!

What does *Hot Flash Financial* urge you to do right now?

STEP 9: Take action right away! Start to increase your contributions to your retirement Stash of Cash.

This involves a few steps. I'll call them STEPS 10 and 11. Let me explain how you do this.

Promise yourself that you will contribute more money to your retirement account, starting *now*. Let your hot flashes remind you of your promise so you will you act on it. Tell your employer or the human resource department to take a bigger percentage of your paycheck out each payday to be automatically deposited into your retirement account.

Now is the time to ask yourself: **How much should I take out of my paycheck to put into my own retirement Stash of Cash?**

Many of us made that decision during those first few days at our new job—and have *never* revisited that decision since then. We never gave it more careful thought, even after years at the same job, getting raises, and so forth. So most of us NEVER INCREASED THE PERCENTAGE OF OUR PAYCHECK or the dollar amount that is DEPOSITED IN OUR RETIREMENT ACCOUNT. It just sits there at 1 percent, or whatever you decided oh so many years ago.

Want a Face Lift for Your "Wrinkles"?

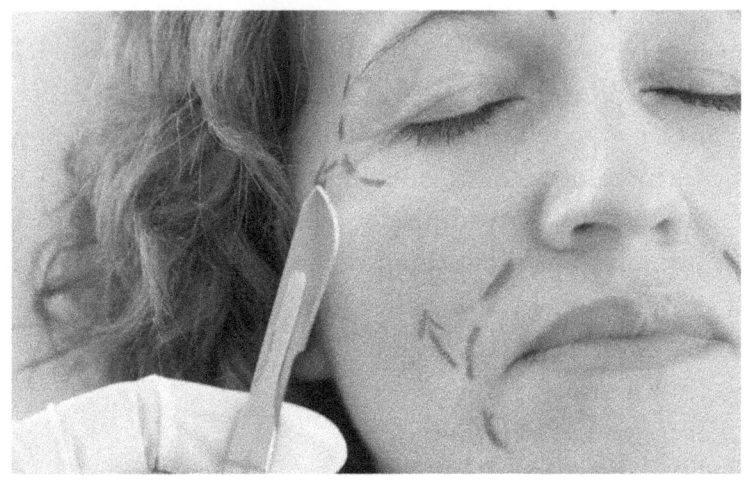

Now here is the really fun part, reserved for us Hot Flash Mamas: if you increase your contributions to the maximum amount, **it is like a BOTOX wrinkle treatment**—*except it LASTS.*

Imagine how big your Hot Flash Stash of Cash would grow if you could work toward increasing your yearly contributions up to $17,500 a year!

Wait, there's more. You can have an even bigger impact on your financial security if you increase your contributions by the **Catch-Up Contribution amount that I discussed earlier.** *If you can do that without going into more debt, DO IT!*

Now, that is a total face lift for the wrinkle in your future financial security.

Hot Flash Financial says, **Now is the time!** That is, now is the time to increase the amount of money you automatically deposit into your retirement account at work.

But increase by how much?

STEP 10: Increase your contributions gradually. Get on your retirement website or go to your human resources director and *increase the amount you take out of every paycheck just 1 or 2 percent right now to begin to fulfill that promise to yourself.*

The first paycheck you might feel a little bite. But you can *adjust your spending* today because you realize **this is a good trade-off.**

At your age you know there are so many TRADE-OFFs in

So give your financial future a face lift, without the pain. Don't go under the knife—take advantage of our miracle compounding cure by increasing your deposits into your retirement account over the next twenty to thirty years. Your goal is to get to the point at which you contribute the maximum legally allowed, and, if possible, the catch-up contribution. Compounding interest will be hard at work, creating miracles in your retirement Hot Flash Stash of Cash. So give yourself the miracle cure for those "unsightly wrinkles," your very own wonderful financial "face lift."

life. The most important ones are the decisions you make about using the money you earn. What will you do with $50 or $80 or $100 (and, for some people, $500) that you could rustle together in a week or a month? Will you use it to increase your financial security? Will you have the strength and smarts to stash it in your retirement account so you will have enough money to pay for everything? Or will you buy more some stuff now?

It is really important to point something out. At your age **you increase your RISK if you** continue to spend your money and **ignore this STEP.** You RISK having too little money in the future. Too little money in your future **can cost you your independence and dignity** and the sweetness of financial security.

You need to build a nice, comfy cushion of cash for yourself. So ask yourself: Can you skip eating at a restaurant once or twice a month? Maybe now is the time to get serious about quitting smoking. Can you go to the hairdresser's every eight weeks rather than every six? Whatever you think might help you add to these contributions. Brainstorm some good ideas.

STEP 11: Create a series of notes in your calendar, about two or three months down the road. Each note will remind you to increase your contribution another 1 or 2 percent. Keep increasing the number of dollars you contribute to your retirement account every three to four months for the next year or so.

This will help you increase the size of your Hot Flash Stash of Cash and so increase your financial security.

IRAs—A Short Discussion

You got smart about your Hot Flash Stash of Cash. Now get even smarter. IRAs are also great accounts for **Hot Flash Stashes**. They are accounts that are held in your name (never jointly). They are also *kept separate* from the accounts you use for daily spending and are *reserved for your future*. And the money is also untouchable. The same set of penalties apply to IRAs as 401(k)s and 403(b)s if you take money out early.

IRAs are a little different from defined contribution plans. You have to open an IRA yourself. But don't worry; it is not hard. You just walk into a bank or an investment house, or you can set up an account online. You fill out a little paperwork, sign it, and then get your account number—easy. The hardest part is making sure you put the money into the account every year. That's up to you.

If you have MAXED OUT on your 401(k) contributions and also deposited up to the legal limit on the Catch-Up Contribution, the IRA is the next type of account you can use to build a nice Hot Flash Stash of Cash account. Oh, and by the way, you can also add a Catch-Up Contribution to an IRA!

If you are not employed but are married to someone who is, let me remind you that you can open a *spousal IRA*.

If you are a self-employed person and earn an income, you can open a *SEP IRA*. SEP is short for Simplified Employee Pension Plan. It allows you, as your employer, to contribute to a traditional IRA.

Even if you have an employer plan, like a 401(k), you can still fill up an IRA because the law has changed to benefit you. So you can build an even larger tax-advantaged Stash of Cash.

IRAs have some of the **same tax benefits** as defined contribution plans. Once you deposit your cash into the IRA, the gains or profits you make are *not taxed*. That is the easy part to tell you. After that, there are a lot of particulars to explain.

So here is the explanation:

You can get a tax benefit, but you have to decide if you want that tax benefit today, when you *put the money in* OR later, when you *take it out* during retirement.

If you want a tax deduction now, that is for the year you deposit your contribution, put the money into a **traditional IRA** (You get a deduction if you earn less than a certain salary figure the IRS publishes). Like a 401(k) or other defined contribution plans, you pay tax when you take the money out to use during your retirement.

If you decide to you would rather get a tax break later, *after* you retire, then deposit money into a Roth IRA. With a Roth IRA, you do not pay taxes on the compounding gains while the money stays in the account (like any retirement account). The benefit of a Roth IRA is that you do not pay tax on any of the money you withdraw from your Roth IRA

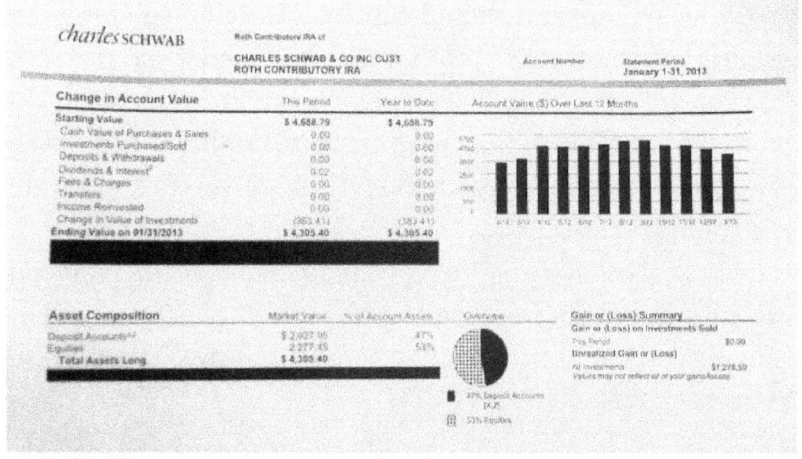

after you retire. If you think tax rates will go up in the next twenty years, you should consider a Roth IRA. Sorry if this is confusing, but so is the tax code.

> Contribute to an IRA in addition to your defined contribution plan each year.

Hot Flash Financial recommends that you contribute to an IRA in addition to your 401(k) each year. Or, if you are a spouse who does not work, contribute to a *spousal IRA*. You can contribute as much as $5,500 to an IRA in 2013. Once again, Uncle Sam wants to be nice to Hot Flash Mamas. So if you are fifty or older, you can contribute, or catch up with an additional $1,000, for a total of $6,500 in 2013.

Make that contribution to your IRA, especially if you have filled up your 401(k) already by contributing the maximum legally allowed plus the Catch-Up Contribution (if you qualify).

> IMPORTANT: **Don't let anyone tell you that you must get a deduction immediately** *for a contribution to your IRA and that otherwise it is not worth it to contribute. That person is wrong, short sighted, and just silly.*

Why wouldn't an extra $1,000 or $6,000 deposited into your account, growing exponentially thanks to compound interest, be a benefit to you?

> *This is the* **TIME** *when* **SIZE MATTERS!**
> *Build that Stash BIG, baby!*

You can have a portion of your paycheck automatically deposited in your IRA, whether it is in an investment house, an online investing service, or another bank. You simply have to deposit your take-home pay in your checking account and tell the bank to deposit a certain amount into your IRA. Or have the service deposit money directly from your employer into an IRA at another institution. The rest is easy.

Make that HOT FLASH STASH OF CASH BIG! Let it grow—put that money to work for you when it is inside that account so it will GROW BIG!

Risk? Did She Say **RISK?**

It is important for you to build up your Hot Flash Stash of Cash. If you do *not,* you **RISK running out of money before you run out of breath.**

We women **RISK living a really long time**. Statisticians say about half of us will live until we are eighty-five. **The other half of us will live longer, well past eighty-five!**

We need money to make sure we have enough to pay **for everything we need thirty to forty years after our hot flashes start.**

Stash that cash in retirement accounts so you do not RISK running out of money when you are eighty years old. When you are that old, you may not feel spry enough to take even a small part-time job.

> *What if you run out of money before you run out of breath?*

The next RISK is that the **cost of groceries and health care are going to go up.** This is called *inflation RISK.* The increase in these prices can really put a crimp in your lifestyle. (In fact, your life might not have any more style.) As inflation increases over the next twenty to forty years, you are likely to discover that your money cannot buy as much as it does today. You may find that you can only afford the basics or, worse, have trouble affording even those.

So build your Hot Flash Stash of Cash over the next few decades. Start to increase your contributions to your very own, personal Hot Flash Stash of Cash. That way you don't leave yourself so open to inflation risk or the risk that you will run out of money before you run out of breath.

> *Remember, you can **never, ever, ever have too much money** in your Hot Flash Stash of Cash. That money will just sit patiently, growing and waiting for you. It will be ready for you to pay for everything you need in your future.*

The Duchess of Windsor, Wallis Simpson, once said, "You can never be too rich or too thin." Well, we women focused on *the wrong clause*. We wanted to be **thin**, so we made ourselves crazy with diets of all types. We hated our bodies and fretted about a little bulge, or even big ones.

Hot Flash Financial wants you to concentrate on the first clause and become more fixated on the amount of money you have in your name rather than the number of pounds on the scale.

At *Hot Flash Financial* I simply say, "You can never be too rich."

Remember, financial security is your goal. Use those Hot Flashes to remind you to take some money from every paycheck and give it to yourself for the future. That way you can build a nice, big, comfy cash cushion that will give you the independence and dignity you deserve for working so hard to build it.

> *Take yourself seriously. And take action. After all, like that commercial says, "**You** are WORTH IT!"*

IN A FLASH—A QUICK SUMMARY

I gave you some great secrets in this chapter. First, I told you where to stash your cash, or at least what types of accounts should be the first you fill as you build your Hot Flash Stash of Cash. What was the reason? You get *amazing* tax breaks. You get to keep more of your paycheck in your own name at the same time that you pay less to the IRS. Second, I encouraged you to increase the size of your contributions gradually. (It would be excellent if you could increase your deposits to the maximum legally allowed, then add the catch-up amount each year.) Whatever you decide, if you follow these STEPS you will get compounding interest to work its magic for you, big time. In addition, you will save more money than most Americans do—you know who they are, the ones with the biggest, ugliest, most unsightly wrinkles in their financial future. Not you. You are smarter than that.

You are giving yourself a "face lift for your finances," so you can increase your financial security, laughing all the way to the bank.

HOT FLASH QUIZ #5

Essay Question:

How can you get a tax break, like the top 1 percent?

Multiple Choice:

1. What is a Spousal IRA?

a. A medical procedure for older married women, performed in sub-Saharan Africa.

b. A euphemism for a sexual position.

c. A retirement account for the spouse of a person who is employed.

2. What is a Trade-Off?

a. I forgo buying a designer bag (for $13,000) and deposit that money into my retirement account for my future.

b. I don't charge $13,000 on my credit card for shoes and an evening dress that Kim Kardashian wore (or was it Snooki?). I would do better if I deposited the cash into my retirement account at work.

c. I deposit the maximum plus a Catch-Up Contribution in my retirement account at work. And I cut back on spending to allow me to make that deposit.

d. None of the above.

e. All of the above.

Fill in the blank with one of the following words:

I need to increase the size of my _____ to make my future more secure.

a. boobs

b. butt

c. lips

d. assets

The Dutchess of Windsor Wallis Simpson influenced the behavior of many women with her simple assertion, "You can never be too rich, or too thin." After carefully reading *Hot Flash Financial,* which clause do you think is more important? Can you stop dieting now?

CHAPTER 6

Lots of Options and More Control

CHAPTER 6 GOALS:

• *Help you make careful decisions about your income during the years you continue to work.*
• *Give you a set of options to increase your control over your own money and your future.*

I have been encouraging you to increase your financial security by building your Hot Flash Stash of Cash. All you need is to do is find **more cash so you can make your Stash a lot bigger.** How? Well, of course I am going to give you some more steps you can take to find this cash. Nevertheless, it is also time to give you some choices. That way, you decide which options will work best for you. Each STEP you take will give you more control over your future as well as your money.

Ready?

STEP 12: Ask for a raise at work.

Research shows that we women are a bit more timid than men are when it comes to asking for a salary increase. We just assume that our boss will recognize our good work and reward it. By contrast, men often ask for raises. That's one reason why most men earn more money than most women. Research shows that we women get about 77 cents for every $1.00 paid to a man. It might be nice to get the same size paycheck as your male colleague down the hall who is doing the same job as you.

If you want to ask for a raise, start by **developing a careful strategy** that is **diplomatic and professional.** You can read Evelyn Murphy's book, *Getting Even.* She encourages you to do your homework before you ask so you know the dollar parameters. She also gives you some ideas to help you build your case for that raise.

A few *Hot Flash Financial* pointers:
• Develop a timetable for the "ask." The timetable has to respect the company's schedule for deciding on pay raises. So start a few months before your boss and his/her supervisors will be discussing pay increases. Be ready before any decisions are made.
• Clarify your contributions to your unit's success and how they have helped the company succeed. Develop a list of everything you did each week and each month that helped you and your boss reach his/her goals and contribute, as they say, to the "bottom line." It should be things like how you exceeded your goals and increased revenues over the last six to twelve months doing x, y, and z, using numbers to show your impact clearly, and how you increased efficiency and helped your project come in on time and under budget. Write your list down neatly, as if it were a résumé. That way you can meet with your boss at the appropriate time to politely and professionally recount your contributions to the unit and the team. Then hand the boss your list so that s/he has a copy to show his/her supervisors as ammunition to argue for your salary increase. After all, this is a negotiation, not a demand.

Another way to help you negotiate for higher pay: get a job offer with a higher salary from another employer. Consider using this as part of your strategy—a bargaining chip. Having this job offer says that your skills are worth more than you are currently getting paid. If you have made a good argument for the reasons your boss needs *you,* s/he may match that raise or beat it. If s/he does not, take the job with the other employer. You'll get a higher income and maybe even a better boss. Make sure you are prepared to leave your current job when you begin this negotiation.

Before you enter your boss's office, develop a script. Turn to someone you trust—outside of work—to role-play your boss. Then practice. Ask for feedback to help you strengthen your position. Then ask your trusted partner to change roles and repeat your argument for a raise back to you. Listen to the way your argument sounds. With what you have just learned, improve your strategy and role-play again.

This takes time and great diplomacy because there is an art to asking for a raise. *Hot Flash Financial* suggests you develop that art to your own advantage. That would certainly be a great way to get more money into your **Hot Flash Stash of Cash.**

But there is another way to get more money.

STEP 13: Get an additional income stream coming into your household.

If you are not working, why not become employed? Or if you have a full-time position and have the strength and the stamina, take on a second or a part-time job. If you are a teacher and have summer vacation, think of getting a job during the summer.

There are so many options. You can tutor throughout the year and/or offer homework help. Post ads in local libraries and public schools as well as private schools. Also consider becoming an SAT prep tutor (www.kaptest.com). If you would like to freelance in your profession (and have not signed a noncompete agreement), go to www.oDesk.com and hit the "find work" button. Or go to www.elance.com to be found by others (with elance you have to "create your own profile").

If you are artistic, you can sell your wares through www.

etsy.com. Odd jobs can be found through www.Craigslist.org and another site called Task Rabbit (www.taskrabbit.com).

These options should provide extra money—something that so many people think they do not have in order to save for your future. Then channel those extra earnings into your Hot Flash Stash of Cash to increase your financial security!

STEP 14: You (and/or your partner) can decide to delay retirement. Take a few more years earning an income. You effectively delay the year of your very last paycheck.

Think about the positive impact of working a few more years beyond sixty-five or sixty-six. You can bring in **more money** while your body and mind are healthy and your Hot Flashes keep you alert and warm. This will give you **more time to build a more secure foundation for your future.** Here are some reasons to do this.

You will likely live longer than your grandparents did, so your employer can pay for part of this increased longevity. By doing so, you will have a lot more income to work with once you do retire. Because you are probably pretty senior in your workplace, you probably earn the biggest paychecks of your lifetime. So why not continue receiving those big paychecks and use them intelligently to become more secure? When you delay retirement, even by just a few years, you give yourself more money and more time to take the needed steps to improve your financial picture.

> *Let those Hot Flashes remind you that you have options.*
> * *Use the extra time and extra money to your advantage.*
> * *Make careful decisions about the date you stop working and the date you start your Social Security benefits.*

STEP 15: Use your additional paychecks intelligently. You have more discretionary income, so deposit more money into your 401(k) and your IRAs as well as any other Hot Flash Stashes of Cash you have.

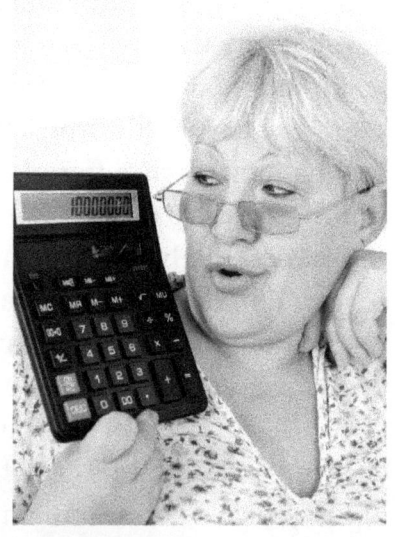

Since you earn more money now than you ever have, use your discretion and deposit more money into your Hot Flash Stash of Cash. When you do this, using the *Hot Flash Financial* "wrinkle reduction treatment" becomes a lot easier. Work toward depositing the Maximum Allowable Amount plus the Catch-Up Contribution—and contribute to your IRAs the additional years you work. The miracle of compounding interest will be working harder for you.

If you delay retirement and work longer, your Social Security payments will be higher. Remember when I told you to look at your Social Security statement? If you delay Social Security until you are seventy, you may receive hundreds of dollars more each month. So work longer if you are healthy. That way delaying Social Security payments is much easier.

Although *Hot Flash Financial* recommends that you take advantage of your ability to work a few more years after age sixty-five, don't forget that **there are pink slips in the twenty-first-century economy.**

Working a few years longer may become a challenge if you work for someone else. Large corporations like to merge and then lay off employees who are considered "redundant." The Great Recession that started with the housing market meltdown then spread into the banking sector pushed a huge number of people out of work. As of the end of 2012, the construction, real estate, and mortgage industries have still not totally recovered, so there are fewer jobs in these sectors than there were before the downturn.

If you have been laid off, it is likely you have not found another position. You may have found yourself in an "unplanned retirement."

Unplanned Retirement

AARP Senior Strategic Policy Advisor Sara Rix tells us that about 40 percent of employed Americans get pink slips before they reach the retirement age they had chosen for themselves.

Retiring before you planned creates a lot of challenges. You are usually forced to make decisions about spending *when you are least prepared to do so*. Maybe your children are in college, or you just purchased a new home, or the value of your house has dropped because the housing bubble burst but your mortgage remained high. As a result, you may find yourself tempted to dip into your 401(k) or other retirement accounts.

You have tough decisions to make. You may not be able to find a job that uses your skills and experience *plus* pays well for them. You often have to decide whether you will take a position that pays less. Many people find this very hard to do. Your ego may be on the line, and the new paycheck may not cover the expenses you had before. Will you take this new job to reduce spending pressures or hold off for a better offer in another position?

That has to be your decision. There are trade-offs, as with any decision. In today's Great Recession these trade-offs can put you between a rock and a really hard place.

But there *are* options, especially if you are not getting the job offers you want.

One option is to **go in business for yourself**, be your own boss. Women who are often in and out of the workforce (because of child care or taking care of an aging parent) become consultants, using their experience as a resource. Some are able to build strong businesses.

Women who have not been employed, either because they initially chose not to do so or because they later left the work force, can start a business as well. Some develop a personal interest or hobby, such as gardening or knitting. They know enough about those pursuits to bring products and services to their customers. Further, they can offer advice and classes to clients who want to improve their own green thumbs or keep their thumbs out of the knitting stitches and on the needles. Others draw on a skill or take some classes so they can provide a service.

Let's explore the option of opening your own business.

STEP 16: You can opt to start your own business.

It is nice to be your own boss. You can develop your own approach and put it into action *your* way. You can use your experience to benefit your own bottom line.

Hot Flash Financial is not a business start-up guide, but I can encourage you to think of the financial side of a new business. After all, finances are what *Hot Flash Financial* is all about.

So you do the dreaming, the brainstorming, and then the careful narrowing down of possibilities. Then get real and develop a plan—a careful plan—often called a business plan. And while you are doing the last careful stages of planning, remember there are challenges as well as possibilities.

The **biggest challenge** is actually making money.

Developing a paying clientele often takes time. This is important to know as you plan to start out. Getting a serious income from a new business generally takes three to five years. You have to do a lot of networking and a lot of marketing to get new customers to come and pay for your services and/or products. So when you develop your business plan, make sure you think about this.

There are many things to say about opening a new business, so I decided to summarize in a list of "Dos and Don'ts" (like you see in the fashion magazines). You'll find the list on page 133. These can help you develop a plan that is realistic and can also help you avoid—or at least overcome—many obstacles.

Remember: don't give up too soon. Opening a business, attracting paying customers—all of this is difficult. Have a cash cushion when you start. Go over your sales figures and pay your bills. Figure out how many services you need to sell to cover your costs. Then give yourself a deadline to reach your goal. Be sure to be doggedly determined to meet your goal.

Now I have been serious too long. Let's play. Here are some easy and cost-effective lines of business that will get you to giggle.

1. You could walk other people's dogs and/or become a pet sitter.

2. You could be a chauffeur and/or a go-fer.
   • Lots of parents need someone to pick up their children and take them to after-school programs.

- Folks who work long hours or are elderly or disabled may need help with other services, like doing laundry, picking up and delivering dry cleaning, preparing meals, doing yard work, or making small repairs.
- You could be something like a "rent-a-mom" for single young men who are successful but have no time to take care of their homes. If you have a son, you know what I am talking about.
- If you have a hobby and the tools to do that hobby, consider working in that area.
- If you can really sew, you can become a seamstress and help every high school girl in town with her prom dress as well as every bride (and every bridezilla) with her gown.

3. Or you could become a saleswoman. Remember how well Lucy did it?

If you decide to start your own business to help you shift gears into the next stage of your life, be patient but also be fiercely focused on increasing your clientele. You will be rewarded for your hard work.

> **Hot Flash Financial** *wants you to think seriously about the impact of losing a steady paycheck. Make intelligent decisions about your income and your future.*

IN A FLASH—A QUICK SUMMARY

Okay, my Hot Flash Mama, you got advice and some choices rather than a set of iron-clad, you-must-do steps to follow. Think of these options opening new doors for you. Decide which options are right for you. Then take some more *Hot Flash Financial* STEPS so you can enjoy the dignity and independence that financial security provides.

HOT FLASH QUIZ #6

1. Where is the best place for you to find money for your Hot Flash Stash of Cash?

a. Your mother's wallet.

b. Your brother's wallet.

c. Borrow it—using your credit card. The one with the highest interest.

d. Your paycheck.

2. If you want more money, what is the best strategy to ask for a raise?

a. Stop your boss in the hall while s/he is running to give an important report to the regional head of the corporation. Grab his/her arm and demand a raise.

b. Make an appointment with your supervisor. Then argue with him/her that you need to get paid twice as much as the girl with the big boobs, not less. Support your claims with gossip about others in the office.

c. Create a plan for asking. Figure out when the supervisors in your company decide on raises. Then, five months before, take notes at every office meeting. Keep a To-Do List (on your desktop or desk) of all important goals, deadlines, and your progress toward them. Leave it out so everyone can see it. Then keep track of your accomplishments, such as getting your most important project completed before deadline and under budget. Then make an appointment to meet with your boss a week or so before supervisors discuss raises. Tell your boss what you have accomplished to improve the productivity of his/her unit. (You can prepare a written list and provide a copy to your boss before you start clarifying your important contributions to the office.) Then politely ask to be considered for a raise.

3. What is your plan for your future?

a. I am going to do like Paris Hilton and that Kardashian girl: I will make a sex tape, let it leak, then sue. Or I will just get royalties off it (and my own reality show). What? You think no one wants a sex tape of a postmenopausal woman?

b. I will buy $20 worth of lottery tickets each day, starting today, to fund my life until I am ninety.

c. My plan? I want to quit work by age fifty-five and tour the world. I do not have much money in my retirement accounts. But I watch commercials, and they tell me I can have a vineyard when I retire.

d. If my money runs out, I will move in with my daughter and her horrible, no-good husband.

e. I haven't given it any thought whatsoever. I better follow the *Hot Flash Financial* steps and laugh my way to greater security.

CHAPTER 7

Okay, My Hot Flash Mama, You Accomplished a Lot!

You faced down your worries and anxieties. You looked your fear straight in the eye. In fact, you put your list of fears right in the bull's eye of a dart board, and you fired away. **You substituted action for paralysis, learning for ignoring.**

And that was just the beginning!

You stuck with me and **learned a lot about money—your money.**

> *You overcame huge obstacles, such as fear and procrastination.*

You know what an asset is. And more importantly, **you know how many assets** *you own and control and have computed* their *total value*. All this is extremely important because **your assets are the foundation for your financial security.**

You also learned that you can never be too rich ~~or too thin~~. So you can take steps to increase the amount of assets you have and improve your chances of living "in the lap of luxury" (or at least in your own home).* **If you increase your** assets and, thus, the size of your **Hot Flash Stash of Cash,** you can **decrease your stress** and increase your confidence that you will be able to pay for everything you need.

I gave you the steps to take and urged you to use the resources you have—your paycheck, tax breaks, and time. I encouraged you to **deploy your remaining paychecks strategically** over the next months and years **by taking maximum legal advantage of retirement accounts and compounding interest** so you could grow your Hot Flash Stashes of Cash at the same time that you reduce your taxable income!

I want you to recognize how you could use time to your advantage. If you decide to **delay retirement,** you could take advantage of the increased years of paychecks to **improve your financial picture**. The more years you work, the more deposits you can make into your retirement accounts, and the higher your contributions can rise each year, the greater

---

* Well, here is the fine print: the odds of living like, say, the Kardashians or even your favorite movie star are pretty low. But living comfortably is a good goal. In fact, that is the goal of *Hot Flash Financial*.

the positive impact on your Hot Flash Stashes of Cash. In addition, the longer you delay retirement, the greater the impact of compound interest on your Stash.

I also told you that **you have a surprising amount of control over the amount of Social Security income you could receive** if you make careful decisions about the timing of your first benefit. I taught you how to read your Social Security statement. I pointed you toward the key information and asked you to decide which dollar figure you would like to receive each month when your benefits start. *Hot Flash Financial* really wants women to know that your decision about **the timing of your first Social Security benefit is one of the most important ones you will make about your financial security.**

So, my Hot Flash Mama, you have learned a lot of new things about money—*your money*—and its place in *your future*. As a result, you see your life and your Hot Flash future differently. I hope I have made a good case for increasing your economic stability and safety. *Hot Flash Financial* has urged you to start—right now—to follow my STEPS. Each STEP will help you increase your financial independence as well as your sense of dignity and self-respect.

> *So now you see your life and your future differently.*

Use your next Hot Flash to spur you to action!

When you feel the heat rising, take another *Hot Flash Financial* STEP to increase your security and reduce your risk.

I am so glad you trusted me and trusted yourself to take really important steps to improve your future financial security.

Don't Stop Here!

This is only the beginning of the next phase of your life. (Your hot flashes are telling you that too. But more on that in another book.) **Enter your next stage equipped with *Hot Flash Financial* knowledge.** You are older and wiser now than you have ever been before, and after reading this book, you are also much more knowledgeable about the ways you can prepare yourself financially for your future.

Surrender to your hot flashes. Let them guide you—or at least remind you—to get smarter about money. Take yourself seriously. Trust yourself to do this. **Do this *for yourself*.** Take the *Hot Flash Financial* STEPS. You don't have to complete every task perfectly, but you do need to do them to improve your future.

Oh, and make sure you laugh.
Laugh a lot.

Glossary

When you learn something new, there are always new words and ideas. I don't want them to be stumbling blocks. So I prepared this glossary to help you understand some of new vocabulary. Flip to the glossary whenever you feel unsure of the meaning of a term.

Account statements. Account Statements are reports from each bank, investment house, and institution that holds your money. They are printed every month or, if there is little activity in the account, every quarter. An account statement tells you a lot, such as (a) the name of the person who owns the account and has a right to its contents, (b) what type of account it is (savings, IRA, etc.), and (c) how much money is in the account on a specific date. The statements also tell you (d) your account number and (f) the name of the institution that holds your assets (bank, E-trade, etc., or a retirement institution like TIAA CREF or Fidelity).

Assets. Assets are resources that have real economic or dollar value. What is more, assets are *your* resources. You own or control them. They include things like savings, retirement, and investment accounts. But there is something even more important about assets: you own them because you expect them to benefit you in the future.

Most of us think of our home as an asset. Actually, most of us buy a home because we expect it to increase in value during the thirty-plus years we own it. So, yes, real estate is an asset. Its value goes up and down with the real estate market—that is true of any asset. Gold goes up and down in value, as does oil and other commodities. Stocks and bonds go up and down in value. Over the long term—very long term, like a decade or two—stocks tend to increase in value.

At this writing, the housing market has recently experienced a dizzying rise in values, and then, in 2008, a plunge back toward earth. Real estate values normally rise at the rate of inflation, but if there is increased demand, they will rise faster than inflation,

The long and the short is this: assets increase in value over time—that is, over a long time.

Balance. As in account balance. This is generally the total amount of money held in a savings, retirement, or investment account. We generally like the account balances to increase in size. However, if the account balance is provided by a credit card or mortgage company, it is generally the total amount of money you still owe; this is sometimes called the "balance due."

Catch-up contribution. The IRS gives tax breaks for contributing money to your retirement account at work. But these tax breaks are so generous that the IRS puts some limits on the total amount we can deposit. Nevertheless, the IRS lets us Hot Flash Mamas, age fifty and above, contribute an additional amount and get an even bigger tax break. It is called a "catch-up" contribution. We, and men age fifty and above, can contribute an extra $5,500 (in 2013) to our retirement accounts at work and an additional $1,000 to our IRA.

CDs (certificates of deposit). Often issued by banks, they work like savings accounts. You deposit a certain amount of money and receive a guaranteed interest rate for a specific period of time (e.g. 3 months, or a year). Unlike a savings account, the money you deposit in a CD is generally "locked up" or untouchable until the end of a term. If you withdraw the money from a CD before the end of the term, you lose interest income and may pay a penalty.

CDs are often considered risk free. The risk is low if they are backed by the U.S. Government and the FDIC. But make sure you verify that a CD has that FDIC backing. Some people were scammed by shysters, who promised to deposit their money in CDs, but actually stole the money deposited.

Compound interest. See pages 58–62.

Equity. This word has a variety of uses and meanings, so here is a kinda generic sense of the word: equity is the part of the asset (or home) that you actually own and paid for so far. If you paid cash for the entire sticker price, your equity equals the value of the asset today. If you used a mortgage or other type of debt to help you pay for the asset (e.g., your home) your equity is much lower than the market price today.

To find the equity in your home, subtract the total balance you owe to a mortgage company (or bank) from the price you receive for your home. In the case of a home that is, say, worth $250,000 today if you were to sell it, your equity includes the down payment ($25,000) you made and any money you have paid down on the mortgage balance (let's say you paid off $10,000 in principal so far). It also includes any gain you have made on the home ($15,000), because the selling price of your home has gone up to $250,000. (Think of the other figure—the mortgage balance—as the amount of your home that the bank owns.)

See also Home Equity Line of Credit.

Federal Reserve. The Federal Reserve is really a Board of Governors whose primary responsibilities are (1) moderate long-term interest rates, (2) help maintain stable prices, and (3) maximize employment. A discussion of what "The Fed" does is a bit too complex for our book, but we did mention the federal government, so we wanted to help you understand its functions just enough to satisfy you at this stage in your learning process. The Fed takes action that influences the going mortgage rate and/or credit card rates.

Financial literacy. A term that is designed to measure the level of knowledge and capability a person has with respect to finance. If you are financially literate, you understand (1) how *compounding interest* works to your benefit when you save and invest. (See chapter 4 so you can be savvy.) In addition, you can distinguish its impact from that of simple interest. (Also see chapter 4.) You also understand the impact of (2) *inflation* on your ability to purchase basic goods. Chapter 5 talks about inflation's impact on prices. But any one of us girls who has lived through the 1970s can remember how inflation cut into your ability to buy anything.

Because there are parallels between the impact of compound interest and inflation, we introduced you to compound interest and encouraged you to use it to your benefit. Inflation increases its impact over time in a parallel manner.

The final marker of financial literacy is an ability to understand the (3) *diversification of risk* and how you can reduce your investment risk by diversifying your investments. We did not talk about risk diversification in this book, my Hot Flash Mama. We can get to it in later publications, if you seem ready for it.

Why should you care if you are financially literate or *il*literate? Well, older Americans, age fifty-plus, tend to be burdened by financial illiteracy. Only half of us can answer simple questions about compound interest, inflation, or risk diversification. Women and minorities are more likely to be in that group of financially *il*literate folks. Why does that matter? Well, those of us in that group don't save enough for retirement. We often hold a lot more credit card debt, and we tend not to develop a financial plan.

Hot Flash Financial was developed to rectify that problem and help you increase your financial literacy. We are going to SAVE you! Keep reading and following our steps.

Home Equity Line of Credit. This is a second mortgage on a home. In this type of loan the borrower uses the equity built up in her home as collateral or security for the loan. The loan is actually just a line of (revolving) credit that the borrower can use if she wants. The interest rate is set by the bank, and it may be an adjustable rate. Homeowners may use this type of loan for a major repair, such as replacing a heating unit or the roof. This allows the homeowner to pay back the loan over six months or a year. When a home is sold, the first mortgage and the home equity line of credit must be paid off before the homeowner receives the gain or equity in her home.

Investment Return. Whether you put your money into a savings account or invest in stocks, bonds, or even a far more risky hedge fund, you generally expect to get (1) your money back plus (2) an additional gain. The gain is called an investment return; it is a percentage of the total amount originally invested. (The amount originally invested is called "the principal," or capital or cost basis.). This percentage can also be called the "rate of return." Although you may expect a gain, it is important to remember that the return can be either a loss or a gain.

Insurance policies. They come in many shapes and sizes. You probably know you can insure a life, a car, or a house. The list goes on.

Life insurance. You should probably know that there are two basic types—term and whole life (sometimes called universal life). In this discussion, I will focus on term life insurance because it is far more common, and affordable.

Term life policies are what you are generally offered through your employer. They are designed to cover a person for a certain number of years (the "*term*"). The price (or "premium") you pay for Term life is determined by your age. When you are young, the premium is very low. But as you get older and closer to death, the premium will become more expensive.

A term life insurance policy only pays a death benefit *if* a death occurs within the "term" of the life of the person insured. The companies are required to honor the contract and pay the death benefit. But few young people actually die while young (or within the term). I have heard that only about 3 or 4 percent of term life insurance policies pay death benefits.

In short, term life insurance is an inexpensive way to insure against the risk of death for a period of time.

When you have children, most men or major bread winners think that buying life insurance is a good idea, just in case. Although an insurance salesperson will give you an option between term life insurance and whole life, which is more expensive but builds savings into the policy at the same time that it offers a death benefit, most couples decide to buy term insurance.

As the children grow older and leave home, a family's needs change. And as the policy holder gets older, the costs or premiums get more expensive, by hundreds and even thousands of dollars At some point it is not really worth it. For this reason, many insured middle-aged people cancel a term life policy held outside of work.

Match, or matching contributions to retirement accounts. This is a contribution some employers offer. The company wants to encourage you to save for your retirement, so it will match the amount of money that you deposit in your retirement account. Sounds good, doesn't it? Because it is. The company will often match your contribution up to 3 percent of your salary. How about that? It is like getting a 3 percent raise in your salary without even asking for it.

To get that additional income, all you have to do is contribute to your retirement account at work. If your employer provides a match, try to contribute—or deposit—at least 3 percent of your salary so that it will be matched. You have to instruct your employer to create a retirement account for you, and you have to tell your employer how much money you want to be taken from your paycheck to be eligible for the match. *Hot Flash Financial* encourages you to contact your HR department or go online to make sure you are contributing. We will also encourage you to contribute more than 3 percent. After all, you can never be too rich.

If your company has a "match," make sure you are receiving it. If you company temporarily suspended its matching program when the economy went into recession, ask HR when and if the company plans to resume the match program. And if your company does not have a matching program, consider a diplomatic way to ask the company to start a match.

Retirement accounts. Defined contribution accounts, also called 401(k)s, 403(b)s, or sometimes 457(b)s, are accounts employers set up to help their employees fund their own retirement. You make a decision about the amount you want to contribute to this type of retirement account. The deposits you make into these accounts are likely to be the major source of income you will use after your paychecks stop, or you retire.

Remember, defined contribution plans are different from pensions. Pensions guarantee an income to you; they are funded by an employer. If you do not work at a company that offers a pension, you become the only person or entity responsible for your income throughout your retirement. If you do not put any money into your defined contribution plan, you are defining a future retirement with very little, perhaps no money.

Hot Flash Financial recommends you use these 401(k), 403(b), and 457(b) accounts as your key Hot Flash Stashes of Cash. (Although they need not be the only Stashes you have or build.) Retirement accounts are perfect Hot Flash Stashes. They are set aside for your future benefit and security. The money you deposit in these accounts is separated from your cash flow and labeled as "reserved for" your future. If you try to take money out of this type of account, you will pay a 10 percent penalty, and you will pay taxes on that money.

We recommend depositing money into your retirement accounts first and then trying to deposit the maximum legally allowed for these types of accounts, because doing so gives you most benefits. You get tax breaks and often a corporate matching contribution.

Other types of accounts, such as savings and/or investment accounts, are also excellent Hot Flash Stashes of Cash, but they don't give the same tax breaks. And you don't get a corporate match. So take advantage of retirement accounts first, then contribute money to these other types of accounts.

(Important financial planning note: retirement accounts are separate from rainy day accounts or other types of accounts, such as the savings account you are using to build up a down payment so you can purchase a home. All of these accounts are great Hot Flash Stashes because they are separate from your cash flow. And you have also labeled them to show the purpose or goal for these funds. Both rainy day accounts and down payment accounts should be in savings accounts, which are protected by the FDIC.)

IRAs, or individual retirement accounts, are additional means to fund your retirement. *You* have to open an IRA account in an institution you select. And *you* have to fund it. There are legal limits on the amount you can deposit in an IRA each year, and these tend to be lower than those for 401(k), 403(b), and 457(b) limits. The IRS defines these limits, and it gives tax breaks on the profits you earn while the money and the investments remain in the IRA.

There are many types of IRAs. We will not bore you with a long list. The most important ones for you to know about are traditional IRAs, Roth IRAs, SEP IRAs, and spousal IRAs.

Traditional IRAs can be funded by anyone who earns an income. You can fund this type of IRA even if you have a defined contribution account at work. (The law has changed to allow you to hold and fund both types of accounts.) If you are not employed but are legally married to someone who is employed, you can open and fund a spousal IRA. With traditional IRAs, whether spousal or your own, you may be eligible for a tax deduction each year you make deposits into your IRA. There are limits on deductibility, and these are based on your income. These limits vary based on whether you are single or married. *Hot Flash Financial* believes strongly that you should deposit into an IRA every year that you have the money and are qualified to do so, even if you do not get a tax deduction for doing so.

Roth IRAs are similar to traditional IRAs, but they offer some really nice tax breaks. Because of this, however, there are limitations on access to them. Roth IRAs do not provide a tax break when you deposit the money into your account (while you are employed). The good news is that Roth IRAs give you a tax break when you take the money out of the IRA, after you are age fifty-nine and a half. If you believe that tax rates are likely to go up over the next ten to thirty years and you qualify, it might be smart to fund a Roth IRA rather than a traditional IRA. But if you think your income will drop a lot when you retire, then the tax break you will get when you are retired won't benefit you very much.

SEP IRAs (*S*implified *E*mployee *P*ension plans) are developed for small business owners. They work pretty much like defined contribution plans (401(k), 403(b), and 457(b) accounts) in the sense that you can contribute higher amounts than traditional or Roth IRAs allow. The tax breaks on your contributions are somewhat different. If you own a small business and have no other employees, a SEP IRA might be the best option for you. If you have employees, you will be responsible for setting up and funding their SEP IRAs.

Now, a *Rollover IRA* is not a technical term. It is one used in advertising to get you to move your 401(k) account to the advertiser's institution (let's call that Institution #2). The process of moving it is called "rolling it over." When done correctly, a rollover will *not* require you to pay a penalty or a tax when you move or roll it over to that new institution.

Why would you do this and how is it done? Well, if you leave your employer, you are eligible to move that money to another financial institution. Your employer's plan usually offers you a set of mutual funds for your retirement investments. Some employers' retirement accounts offer access to excellent funds; others offer mediocre funds or mutual funds with less than average performance. So you can move your retirement account to an IRA, where you will have an unlimited number of options for investment.

How do you roll over your retirement account? Usually you open a traditional IRA at another institution, our Institution #2. Remember that you hold your retirement funds through an employer; the retirement account is managed by another institution, often Fidelity. We will call that Institution #1. To roll over your accumulated assets in the employer account, you generally make a request to Institution #1, telling that institution that you want to *roll over* your account to Institution #2. Institution #1 will then sell all of your mutual funds at no cost to you, and it will mail you a check for the entire amount and/or wire the money to your new IRA account at Institution #2. If you receive the check, you must deposit the entire amount in the new IRA at institution #2 within sixty days—or else you pay taxes and a penalty.

IRS. The Internal Revenue Service. It receives taxes from individuals and uses that money to pay for the federal government's programs—everything from inspecting meat you eat to launching rockets into outer space.

Online access to accounts. Most financial institutions in the twenty-first century will allow you, as an account holder, to view your accounts online. You will need a username and password. And you will probably have to notify the institution that you want to set up online access.

Why does an institution that guards your money make you jump through so many hoops? Because the bank or investment institution wants to make absolutely sure that they are allowing YOU access to your accounts, not some thief. So they are likely to make you go through a series of steps to keep your accounts safe from hackers and other nefarious persons. (Remember, they asked Jesse James why he robbed banks. He said, "Well, that is where the money is." If a modern-day Jesse James wanted to rob a bank, he would probably go where the money is—online. He could get money wired from your account to his own.

Tell the branch office of your bank you want online access. Follow their rules. They may need to send you a letter acknowledging your right to start online access. And that letter may have a temporary password, one that lasts a few days or weeks. That will keep hackers away. In addition they may have strange and complicated ideas of the password that you can use. Why? Because they want to keep your account secure. So follow the steps they require, and use their services. Online access allows you to find out how much money you have in each account, transfer money from one account to another, and so forth. And you don't have to leave the comfort of your own home. In addition, you can download statements and add up how much money you have, say, on your birthday, on New Year's Day—any day. Finally, online access makes it really easy to create an updated list of your assets every year.

Reverse mortgage. This is a special type of loan sold to homeowners who are aged sixty-two or older. This type of loan allows homeowners to draw on a percentage of the equity they have accumulated in their home. So it is a special type of home equity loan. By 2012 very few homeowners have secured reverse mortgages.

The reverse mortgage is different from a regular mortgage. In a reverse mortgage, interest is added to the loan balance each month so that the size of the loan balance grows. The loan has to be repaid either when the borrower sells her home, she moves out, or she dies.

How do reverse mortgages work? Let's start by reminding you how most mortgages work. In a *traditional mortgage* you pay off your mortgage over a number of years. As you pay down the traditional mortgage, the loan balance drops and the amount of equity that you hold grows.

In a *reverse mortgage* you borrow against this equity. So your loan balance grows over time. You could say that the process works "in reverse."

Reverse mortgages were developed for homeowners who have little income but a lot of equity locked up in their home. If you want to continue to live in your home, this can be one option you can consider. But you could face foreclosure, if you run out of money and do not pay (1) your property taxes, (2) your insurance, or (3) other expenses in the future.

Reverse mortgages have come under criticism for charging high fees and offering homeowners access to small percentages of the equity in their homes. In response to these criticisms, there are two distinct types. A "Saver" reverse mortgage allows you to borrow less, but you pay lower fees and lower costs. The "Standard" reverse mortgage has higher fees but allows you to borrow more money.

You can use other options instead of a reverse mortgage to gain access to more money for your support. The most effective approach is to sell your home (rather than obtain a reverse mortgage.) Use the equity to buy a less expensive home (with lower property taxes, insurance costs, utility costs, etc.) and reserve the remaining amount to pay for living expenses.

Another option to consider is quite simple: lower your expenses. State and local programs can help you defer property taxes, lower heating costs, and/or save on other bills. And you may be able to refinance an existing traditional mortgage to lower your monthly expenses.

If, after reading these comments and cautions, a reverse mortgage looks like a good option for you, please don't rush into signing the paperwork. It is usually a good idea to wait, until your late sixties or well into your seventies. Because the debt burden increases the longer you have a reverse mortgage, it is wise to wait. Another point to consider: think carefully about your payout options. If you just get a line of credit through your reverse mortgage, you only pay interest on the money you draw out. There is another option called a "monthly payout." This is a good option if you need additional income for expenses each month. The third option, a "lump sum" payout, holds the most risk. If you borrow a lot of money in a lump sum, you will be responsible for the interest on this large sum of cash. Be absolutely sure you need all of that money immediately. You might prefer to take out a line of credit, also called a home equity line of credit, instead of a reverse mortgage.

Social Security benefits. You have a right to Social Security benefits—that is, a monthly check—if you have worked for at least ten quarters, or two and a half years. You have to make a decision about the year you start your benefits. This is one of the most important decisions you will make, so think about it carefully. Read the discussion in chapter 3 to understand your most important and basic options.

Unplanned retirement. This occurs when employees, age forty-five or older, lose their jobs. Whether it is a corporate merger, acquisition, or massive layoff in the private sector or government jobs, this drastic change can have dire consequences. During the Great Recession many did not another job, so they found themselves in retirement before they had planned to stop working. They often have mortgage payments and other high expenses to meet. As a result, they have to make very tough decisions.

Resources

We welcome you to the *Hot Flash Financial* website. There are loads of things to do on our site. Here is our link: **hotflashfinancial.com**.

Get your very own **List of Assets** and your own "math slave." Download our List of Assets table from the Hot Flash Financial Site: **http://hotflashfinancial.com/tools/list-of-assets/**

You will probably need to have access to software that creates spreadsheets, called Excel. But if you have a child or grandchild familiar with this type of software program, that child can probably download it into a program that works with your operating system.

On the Internet

There are other sites that offer excellent advice. We select sites developed by professional organizations and research institutes. So you don't have to worry about being "sold" something, like the financial equivalent of a ShamWow!

Take a rainy or snowy day to explore these sites. They are goldmines.

smartaboutmoney.org Developed by NEFE, the National Endowment for Financial Education. A related site is myretirementpaycheck.org.

mymoney.gov The Financial Literacy and Education Commission has brought together financial advice offered by twenty-one federal entities. This includes a special set of resources for women: mymoney.gov/category/topic1/women.html.

- I am particularly fond of the US Department of Labor's downloadable book *Taking the Mystery out of Retirement Planning,* found at dol.gov/ebsa/publications/near retirement.html. The pictures are a bit cute. The recommendations are top quality.
- I also like the new Consumer Financial Protection Bureau: consumerfinance.gov. It is staffed by highly trained professionals who offer a wealth of information to Americans. The CFPB updates its site regularly with important information. They have a section devoted to financial protection for "Older Americans": consumerfinance.gov/older-americans. And they have a great link to other sites that help you protect your investments, avoid scams, and find help for elder financial abuse. These include the North American Securities Administrators Association's Senior Investor Resource Center: nasaa.org/1723/senior-investor-resource-center. They really zoom into elder fraud and financial exploitation.

Boston College's Center for Retirement Research has a great set of sites. The material from the Financial Security Project is fun.

Their financial security project has a few great sites: http://fsp.bc.edu/target.

- Managing your money in retirement: http://fsp.bc.edu/managing-your-money-in-retirement.
- An interactive program to help retirees develop a plan: http://fsp.bc.edu/target-your-retirement.
- And a fun interactive tool called Curious Behaviors. It gets you to make choices and shows you how our human "DNA may get in the way": http://fsp.bc.edu/target-your-retirement.

CRR also offers a great Social Security Claiming Guide that you can read as an e-book or download: http://crr.bc.edu/wp-content/uploads/joomla/claiming_guide/claiming_guide__rev_0706.pdf.

And a new piece called Working Longer: http://crr.bc.edu/special-projects/books/working-longer/.

Don't miss the excellent blog called Squared Away. http://squaredawayblog.bc.edu/. It has excellent discussions of key issues facing you, your friends and family. Many of the blogs focus on issues that are crucial for those of us facing retirement. Sign up today so you can keep informed when each blog is released.

There is great information hidden in some unexpected places:

The Society of Actuaries Hmmm, bet you didn't think of looking there. How about "Women Take the Wheel: Destination Retirement," which you can find going to soa.org/research/research-projects/pension/research-managing-retirement-decisions.aspx. There are other strong publications to download that can be accessed by reviewing the list and selecting topics like, "Where to Live in Retirement" or "Securing Health Insurance for the Retirement Journey," and so forth.

Women's Institute for a Secure Retirement, or WISER Women, has some excellent information prepared for you. The link will open up a great set of resources: wiserwomen.org. WISER also offers a great publication called "Six Things You Need to Know about Social Security": wiserwomen.org/pdf_files/ebook/chapterfour.pdf. Don't stop there. Keep exploring WISER's website. It is very rich.

The Retirement Resource Center offers guidance from experts that is untainted by business. Like a dentist or doctor who offers expertise, the Retirement Resource Center charges a fee for its advice, but it is nominal, like a copay: retirement-resource-center.com/retirement-education-resources-for-consumers-and-employees.

OWL (Older Women's League, the voice of midlife and older women) has great information about Social Security. They devote an entire website to Social Security Matters. Go right to the page called Get the Facts: socialsecuritymatters.org/Get_the_Facts.html. OWL starts off by answering the important question: Will Social Security be there for us? It offers facts, such as Social Security has a surplus of $2.6 trillion, and clarifies that Social Security is fully funded for thirty years. Take a look at this site and the other work done by OWL.

AARP has publications for women on Social Security: aarp.org/work/social-security.

Social Security is a really important resource for "women of a certain age." Many women receive a good portion of their income from Social Security. So read as much as you can about Social Security. And make sure you exercise all of your rights to this government benefit.

The Social Security website devotes considerable attention to women. They break down the information so that you can click on links that are appropriate for you. So go to this page http://www.socialsecurity.gov/women/#a0=-1 and click on one of the following options: working woman, or a bride, a wife, a divorced woman, a caregiver or a widow. Finally, they have a whole section for women who receive social security benefits.

You might want to start with the very uplifting (& short) video created by the National Academy of **Social Security, called Social Security: just the facts.** http://www.nasi.org/learn/social-security/just-the-facts. Click on the blue text with the name of the video.

Then get down to brass tacks:

You can get an estimate of the income benefits that Social Security will provide you: http://www.ssa.gov/estimator/. Make sure that you are on the "*official website of the U.S. Social Security Administration*" when you input the information required. And always be careful about sharing your social security number with *anyone*, online or off.

And if you are interested in thinking about safety-net issues a little more, go to the **National Academy of Social Insurance** to learn a bit more about Medicare, long-term care, unemployment insurance, and worker's compensation and disability: nasi.org/learn.

Real estate Get estimates of the current value of your home. Go to www.trulia.com for an estimate of the value of your home. Click on **Estimates** on the home page. Type in your address.

Trulia seems to give you an estimate based on the recent listing prices in the neighborhood, although they may give you an average price for the area. There are other websites that provide this information. They include www.redfin.com and www.zillow.com.

You can also use websites to explore the costs of housing in other areas of the country or your state.

Here is some inspiration to help you save more of your paycheck. I like to recommend nonprofits and professional organizations for advice. They are not selling anything; they just give good advice.

ASEC.org has some wonderful savings tips.
- choosetosave.org/tips/index.cfm?fa=display&content_ID=3533. And they also have some warnings, like "Top Savings Mistakes" (on the same page).
- See, also there, "Practical Savings Tips for Every Day Savings": choosetosave.org/tips/index.cfm?fa=display&content_ID=3539.
- There are also savings tips for your utilities: choosetosave.org/tips/index.cfm?fa=display&content_ID=3542.

The US Government has some fabulous resources. The main site is mymoney.gov.
- Try the FDIC Consumer News. There are great ideas for spending less, and others for saving more: fdic.gov/consumers/consumer/news/cnwin0809/. This includes "Managing your Money in Good Times and Bad." As you can imagine, there is information on borrowing wisely, and protecting against fraud.
- There is "66 Ways to Save Money" from the Federal Trade Commission: ftc.gov/bcp/edu/pubs/consumer/general/gen14.pdf.
- They have a great set of resourses on savings. Try the short video; it encourages you to save more and shows how compounding works: http://www.dol.gov/dol/media/webcast/20110916-ebsa/20110916-ebsa-retirement.htm.
- The Department of Labor has some great brochures and information on the internet. Try "Taking the Mystery Out

of Retirement Planning": dol.gov/ebsa/publications/near-retirement.html.
- The DOL also has a brochure entitled, "Women and Retirement Savings" just for us girls: dol.gov/ebsa/pdf/women.pdf.
- And the DOL has a brochure called, "Savings Fitness": dol.gov/ebsa/pdf/savingsfitness.pdf.

If you smoke, here's another reason to quit, and improve your life and lifestyle. Use the Cost Calculator at http://smokefree.nhs.uk/quit-tools/calculate-the-cost/. Or try a calculator that shows you how much money **you could save** and invest in your Hot Flash Stash of Cash. It also shows you how this will grow—thanks to compound interest: endthehabit.com/content/calculator.htm.

Blogs

Squared Away is an excellent blog: http://fsp.bc.edu/squared-away-blog. And it has a new financial education website: http://crr.bc.edu/special-projects/interactive-tools/squared-away-the-crr%E2%80%99s-new-financial-education-website.

Don't miss **Alicia Munnell's weekly blogs on SmartMoney**: http://blogs.marketwatch.com/encore/search/alicia%20munnell/?s=alicia+munnell&mg=blogs-sm.

While we are listing blogs, take a look at **CBS's MoneyWatch for Work by Steve Vernon**: cbsnews.com/1770-5_162-0.html?query=steve+vernon&tag=srch&searchtype=cbsSearch&tag=mwuser.

Books

A trip to the PUBLIC library or an online check of YOUR public library inventory, can help you reserve and read any book. I probably don't need to remind you that a library card is free, and so is borrowing the book. A nice investment of time, but not cash.

If you want to curl up with a book, we want you to know we are great fans of **Jane Bryant Quinn**. Try reading *Making the Most of your Money* or *Smart and Simple Financial Strategies for Busy People*. Or check out her website: http://janebryantquinn.com.

Evelyn Murphy, *Getting Even* An oldie but a goodie is Barbara Stanny's *Secrets of Six Figure Women.* She also wrote *Prince Charming Isn't Coming.* Although it may seem dated, I still like it.

Roger Fisher, William Ury, and Bruce Patton, *Getting to Yes.* This important book teaches negotiation in general. It is based on the work of the Harvard Negotiation Project.

The *Forbes* article recommends a book I have not read. But it may be good to consult. It is called ***Crucial Conversations: Tools for Talking When the Stakes Are High.***

Hot Flash Extra!
New Business Do's & Don'ts

As promised, here is my list of things to consider when you want to start a business.

Read the list of Do's to help you develop a plan that will work for you. Then read the second list—a set of cautions—to help you avoid common pitfalls. If you become aware of the obstacles faced by those who preceded you, you are less likely to make the same mistakes. And, you can tighten up your business plan and move toward success.

DO

• Develop a business that draws on your expertise and on your existing skills. (However, if you have signed a noncompete contract, look carefully at the legal limitations on what you can do. The last thing you want is an old employer suing you after they let you go.)
• Try to start up with something that allows you to have a home office, use your existing cell phone, and car.

- Contact professionals to ask their advice. Find out everything you can. They may be able to help with suppliers or transport or make recommendations about the use of technology.
- Develop a formal business plan.
- Clarify what you will sell and how it benefits your customers.
- Plan the way you will market your products or services.
- Figure out how much your inventory, training, and so forth will cost. Also develop a careful, realistic estimate of the amount of time you will need to sell your inventory or make money on the services you provide. Determine your break-even point.
- Build a market for your services, skills, or product. **This is probably the hardest challenge of a new business—finding paying clients.** New business owners always underestimate the time and effort required to build a clientele (kinda like when you have your first child). Marketing is more important than you think, especially during the early stages of a business.
- Use the Internet. There are ways to advertise that don't cost much:
    - If you have a product that looks good in pictures, go to PINTEREST and post it, as others do.
    - Comment on blogs that focus on your area of service or expertise. Make a name for yourself that way.
    - Create a Twitter profile.
    - Create a Facebook page for your business and encourage your friends and family to "LIKE" it.
    - Make a video of the benefits of your service or product, then post it on YouTube.
- Use local fairs, especially fund-raising fairs. Offer to donate your services to an auction/fundraiser—this is free ad-

vertising. And if there is more than one bidder, call the other people vying for the product and offer your services to them.
• You can also combine these strategies with a more traditional approach. Try giving discount coupons for the first customers or price breaks if a client refers a friend.
• Word-of-mouth can be very powerful.
• Figure out what your competition is doing, and then do it better.
• Find out the market rate for services like yours so you can charge appropriately.

DON'T
• Don't invest a lot of money in your new business initially. Avoid investing in large machines, rental space, or inventory until you have a good income from your new business.
• Don't reinvent the wheel. Learn from experienced professionals how they started out, what they did right, and what they did wrong.
• Don't fly blind. A careful business plan can help you understand how much money you will need to start your business and then maintain it during your first year or two as you gain momentum.
• Don't get caught with too little money to cover your personal costs and income.
• Don't expect your business to turn a good profit the first year.
• Don't sit around waiting for customers to find you and your product or service. Your job from day one is to find customers and clients.
• Don't underprice your services, and don't overprice them either. Many women charge too little for their work and are often embarrassed to ask for what they deserve.

About the Author

Wendy Weiss earned her MBA in finance from Brandeis University's International Business School, in 2001. She used this training to start offering financial advice at Morgan Stanley, then at Banc of America Investment Services, Inc. (now, Merrill Lynch). During her first decade in this field, she worked to increase financial literacy, developing a curriculum on managing "risk" (longevity risk, market and inflation risk) as well as contributing to a review of the U.S. Department of the Treasury's Financial Literacy and Education Commission's proposal. She was invited to join the sophisticated *Post-Retirement Needs and Risks* study group of the Society of Actuaries (SOA). As a result, she coauthored papers on "Income During Retirement, and "Housing Options" in the SOA publication *Decisions before Retirement*. And she contributed to another SOA publication: "The Impact of Retirement Risk on Women." She continues to offer intelligent advice to her readers so they can make informed decisions about their money and their future.

www.ingramcontent.com/pod-product-compliance
Lightning Source LLC
Chambersburg PA
CBHW020908090426
42736CB00008B/542